Jacob V. Little

What the Bible tells us about the Location of Heaven and Hell

And the first, second, and third coming of Christ

Jacob V. Little

What the Bible tells us about the Location of Heaven and Hell
And the first, second, and third coming of Christ

ISBN/EAN: 9783337171650

Printed in Europe, USA, Canada, Australia, Japan

Cover: Foto ©ninafisch / pixelio.de

More available books at **www.hansebooks.com**

WHAT THE BIBLE TELLS US

ABOUT THE

LOCATION OF HEAVEN AND HELL

AND THE

First, Second, and Third Coming of Christ.

BY JACOB V. LITTLE,
Author and Owner.

PUBLISHED BY
JACOB V. LITTLE,
DECKERTOWN, N. J.

1890.

Entered according to act of Congress,

By Jacob V. Little,

In the year 1889, in the office of the Librarian of Congress, at Washington.

(*All rights reserved.*)

PRESS OF
JENKINS & McCOWAN,
224-228 CENTRE ST.

CONTENTS.

	PAGE
PREFACE	7
1.—THE LOCATION OF THREE HEAVENS	13
2.—WHAT THE BIBLE TELLS US ABOUT THE LOCATION OF HELL	29
3.—THE FIRST COMING OF CHRIST TO MAKE A SACRIFICE FOR SIN	81
4.—CHRIST'S SECOND COMING; TO BE A KING AND THE PRINCE OF PEACE	93
5.—CHRIST'S THIRD COMING; TO BE THE LION OF THE TRIBE OF JUDAH	132
6.—A REVIEW OF THE SUBJECTS IN VERSE	173

PREFACE.

WE are taught in the Word of God that Jesus when he was on the earth gave men more credit for *believing* what he said, and what the prophets had told them, than he did for anything they did. If we love our Redeemer for what he has done for us, we should believe all he has told us in his Word. When Jesus told the centurion he would heal his servant, and the centurion told him to "Speak the word only, and my servant shall be healed," Jesus said, "I have not found so great faith, no, not in Israel." (Matt. 8 : 10.) Then Jesus said, "As thou hast believed, so be it done unto thee." In view of this, we may ask the question, Would not Christ and the Holy Spirit make the preaching of his gospel more successful than it is if the preachers would believe, and explain to the people more of the prophetic or revealed part of the Bible?

All the prophets have said about the future history of the world is as plain as what they have said about its past history. And the literal fulfillment of prophecy in the past should prove to us that all the prophets have said as to what will be done on the earth will be fulfilled in the same way.

We obey the Lord if we believe his words, and

the evil spirit if we do not believe what the Lord has revealed to us. Satan blinded men, and they did not believe the preaching of Noah, and the same spirit prevented men from believing on Christ, and he will while the Lord permits him to do it, and while men are fools enough to be deceived by him, and refuse to believe what the Lord has told them, and will not accept the sacrifice Christ has made for sin. The Jews offer no sacrifice, and will not believe on the one Christ has made for them. That spirit is called "the god of this world," and he is controlling all men to a greater or less extent, and he will not let men believe that the Lord will do what he has told us he will do in the future. Do we believe more prophecy than the Jews do? Christ has well said, " O fools·and slow of heart to believe all that the prophets have spoken." (Luke 24 : 25.) " Professing themselves to be wise, they became fools." (Rom. 1 : 22.) "The lion hath roared: who will not fear? The Lord God hath spoken: who can but prophesy?" (Amos 3 : 8.) And who is man that he should refuse to believe the Lord's prophets? Suppose a friend told us he would do four things. If we told him we believe he would do two, and not the other two things he had promised to do, what credit would that friend give us for believing his word? Our faith in the Word of God should include all he has promised to do. We will never understand the Bible until we are *willing* to believe it.

The prophets had told the Jews how long they

would be in Egypt and in Babylon. Christ told them "the temple would be thrown down" (Matt. 24 : 2), and that would end the Jewish sacrifice. Then he said, "Blindness, in part, is happened to Israel till the fullness of the Gentiles comes in." (Rom. 11 : 25.) They are blind to what is said about Christ's first coming, and we are blind to all that has been said about his second coming. The Jews and Gentiles should correct this mistake. Faith is the window that will let in the light, or the Holy Spirit, to drive out the darkness so that we can see, hear, and understand the truth. I ask the reader to excuse me for calling the devil and his home by the old names, for I do not think they deserve new ones, and the Lord has not changed them.

I think this book will instruct, and do the common people good. For "the common people heard Christ gladly." (Mark 12 : 37.) But "the chief priests and elders sought false witness against Jesus to put him to death." (Matt. 26 : 59.) It is as hard a task in our day as it was in the days of Christ to change the views of men whose minds have been molded in our theological schools.

That class of men may oppose this work; they will do it as Peter said the "Jews and their rulers did, through ignorance." (Acts 3 : 17.) It is the same evil spirit that darkens the mind now, and keeps out the light of the Holy Spirit. "He that believeth and is baptized shall be saved." (Mark 16 : 16.) Who has told us where to stop believing the Word of God?

Many, in our day, who think they believe and obey enough of God's Word to take them to heaven, and say that is all they want, may, like the Jews, be mistaken. We have worldly wise men who think they can remove their burdens, or free themselves from sin, by what they call good works. Paul said, "Though I bestow all my goods to feed the poor, and though I give my body to be burned, and have not charity, it profiteth me nothing." (1 Cor. 13 : 3.) That charity is the spirit of Christ. "If any man have not the spirit of Christ, he is none of his." (Rom. 8 : 9.) We should ask ourselves the question, Does our knowledge of the Bible and our willingness to believe and obey the commands prove to us that we have the spirit of Christ? If the Holy Spirit has revealed to me the truths presented in this book as recorded in the Bible, and given me light to see, and wisdom to understand, believe, and explain them, and has made me believe it is my duty to publish them to all men, the Holy Spirit will never persuade men not to believe what is revealed, and the evil spirit could have no interest in this work. I will say to all, Do not condemn this book until you know by what authority you do it. Have we a right to say that what the Lord has revealed should not be proclaimed to all men? Peter wanted to take some things from the word of the Lord, and Christ told him it was Satan that wanted that done; and the evil spirit will condemn this book. For that spirit persuaded men to reject the preaching of Christ at his first coming.

And some who claim to be preachers and teachers of God's truth may help him in his work to blind men on this subject. I will do my work. The promise is to the faithful; while we have no power to make our work successful, the spirit will instruct if men are willing to be instructed. We can know the spirit by its *fruit*.

1890.   JACOB V. LITTLE.

THE LOCATION OF THREE HEAVENS.

LET us see what the Bible tells us about the unbounded space it calls heaven. "In the beginning God created the heaven and the earth." (Gen. 1 : 1.)

That part of heaven is the air God created around the earth. It moves with the earth in its rapid flight in space, and without it this world would be a barren waste, and life on earth would end. It belongs to this earth, and is our first heave-up, or heaven. "And God made two great lights ; the greater light to rule the day, and the lesser light to rule the night ; he made the stars also. And God set them in the firmament of heaven to give light upon the earth." (Gen. 1 : 16, 17.) The sun gives light on the earth now, and it must move with it in space, or we could see the change. From this we learn God created the air and called it heaven. He does not say he made the second heaven, in which he created the sun, moon, and stars; and we may be safe in saying that is empty space, in which there is nothing created that could interfere with the rapid flight of the earth and all other planets which revolve around the sun, the centre of this solar system. That part of space would be the second heave-up from the earth, and we must go beyond that to find the space the Bible calls the third heaven, paradise, and the present seat of Christ's kingdom. And the third heaven may be some creation in that part of space around this system of planets, that is of as much use to it as the air is to the earth. The first heaven, or air, at the third coming of Christ will burn, or be changed to a new heaven that will not need the light of the sun. For the glory of the Lord will give it light. But the sun will remain in the centre of this system.

"The heavens, being on fire, shall be dissolved, and the elements shall melt with fervent heat; nevertheless we, according to his promise, look for a new heaven and a new earth wherein dwelleth righteousness." (2 Pet. 3 : 13.)

"And I saw a new heaven and a new earth, for the first heaven and the first earth were passed away, and there was no more sea." (Rev. 21 : 1.) We learn from this that the first heaven, and not the second, will burn or be changed from what it is to a new heaven after the last resurrection.

Paul said he "was caught up to the third heaven, whether in the body or out of the body I cannot tell : God knoweth. How that he was caught up *into* paradise, and heard unspeakable words which it is not lawful for a man to utter." (2 Cor. 12 : 2-4.)

We learn from this that Paul must have left his earthly body, and was then in paradise. He had a body which he did not know from his earthly body, and heard what was said by those in heaven, but he had no right to tell his fellow-men what he had learned about heaven.

Jesus said, "He descended first into the lower parts of the earth. And he is the same also that ascended up far above all heavens." (Eph. 4 : 9, 10.)

"For Christ is entered into heaven itself, now to appear in the presence of God for us." (Heb. 9 : 24.) "And suddenly there was with the angels a multitude of the heavenly host." (Luke 2 : 13.) They came to the earth to tell men that the Lamb of God had come, and that "Christ is a high priest, made higher than the heavens." (Heb. 7 : 26) His Father's throne is higher than the third heaven, which is around this system of worlds.

"And it came to pass, while he blessed them, he was parted from them and carried up into heaven." (Luke 24 : 51.) From this we learn there is a place in space, separate from the earth and all planets in this system, called the third heaven. It is the home of Christ, the angels and the redeemed, and they have been, and are, in communication with men who live on the earth.

One of the malefactors who was crucified with Jesus said to him, "Lord, remember me when thou comest into thy kingdom. And Jesus said unto him, Verily I say unto thee, To-day shalt thou be with me in paradise" (Luke 23 : 42, 43) ; or into the third heaven. Jesus said, "In my Father's house are many mansions; if it were not so, I would have told you ; I go to prepare a place for you." (John 14: 2.) I think these mansions are spiritual bodies that will be given to all the redeemed when they go to heaven, and does not refer to heaven as a place that will have mansions or houses like unto those we have on earth. "Jesus said unto them, Destroy this temple, and in three days I will raise it up. He spake of the temple of his body." (John 2 : 19–21.) "Ye are God's building." (1 Cor. 3 : 9.) "Ye are the temple of God, and the spirit of God dwelleth in you. If any man defile the temple of God, him shall God destroy, for the temple of God is holy, which temple ye are." (1 Cor. 3 : 16, 17.) The above refers to our earthly body. And again: "For we know that if our earthly house of this tabernacle were dissolved, we have a building of God, a house not made with hands, eternal in the heavens. For in this we groan, earnestly desiring to be clothed upon with our house which is in heaven." (2 Cor. 5 : 1, 2.) The above quotation refers to a spiritual body. If our earthly body is a building or temple, our spiritual body could be called a mansion that we could occupy forever in heaven. Angels have come to the earth in spiritual bodies, and they could not be seen by men, and they have come in what appeared to be a human body. The Lord can change them in a second from one to the other.

"By the word of the Lord were the heavens made." (Psa. 33 : 6.) This speaks of more than one heaven that the Lord made, and must refer to the third heaven, for He has not told us he created the second heaven, or empty space, for nothing is created in it. "Behold, the heaven and the heaven of heavens is the Lord's." (Deut. 10 : 14.) "Is not God in the height of heaven? and behold the height of the stars, how high they are." (Job 22 : 12.) Many of them are above our third heaven. "Thick clouds are a covering for him; and he walketh in the circuit of heaven." (Job 22 : 14.) All heavens are in a circuit, and the third heaven is around this solar system. "The sun, moon, and stars are called the host of heaven"—are in the second heaven. (Deut. 17 : 2.) Some do not want to know in this life anything about the future state or our future home. The Creator has ordered the Bible written to instruct us in this life. It will be of no use to us in a future state. And all he has told us about heaven and the home of the lost is of interest to us, to induce us to prepare for the one and escape from the other. Heaven, and the company we expect to meet in heaven, should attract us, and it should be of interest to us to know all the Lord has said about it. If we read, believe, and want to understand what is said about heaven in the Bible, we can do so.

We learn from the Bible that the home of the angels and the redeemed is not on this earth, or in the air, or first heaven, which is all around the earth. And their home could not be in empty space called the second heaven, for that is space prepared for the sun, and the planets which revolve around it. But in the third heaven God could create something in space around this solar system that would supply all the wants of his angels, and the redeemed who are in heaven. It would be the first space in this system that would be suitable for Christ's kingdom. And heaven must be in this system, and move with it in space, or we would soon leave it.

We will see what the astronomers tell us about the movement of the heavenly bodies; that will help us understand what the Bible tells us about heaven, its location, and its movement in space. They prove to us that they know the movement and the rate of movement of all the planets in this solar system, and also the movement of the system. They prove it by telling when a planet will pass between the sun and the earth. They also tell us when the eclipse will occur, and on what part of the earth it will be visible, and the minute it will come on and pass off; and they tell us what part of the sun it will shade, and when there will be an eclipse of the moon. And when a comet comes in sight of the earth, they tell us its rate of movement, and tell us when it will come in sight of the earth again, if it takes a hundred years or more to complete the circuit. If we believe what is revealed to us in the Bible, and all that is explained and proved to us by the astronomers about unbounded space around us, we need not worship an " unknown God," or go to an unknown heaven, or say we do not know where it is.

The astronomers tell us they can see stars so far off in space that it would take light, moving at the rate of 185,000 miles in a second, 60,000 years to reach us. And if they could be taken from this earth to that star they could see in the same direction a firmament no less rich and splendid than that which they beheld from this earth. They tell us these worlds are divided into systems, the members of which are bound together by mutual attraction. Each system has a central sun around which the other members, called planets, revolve. While this revolution is going on, the suns themselves, with their respective planets, move about a common fixed central point.

The earth we inhabit is a planet belonging to what is known as the solar system, of which the sun is the centre. The diameter of the sun is 852,000 miles. Placed where the earth is, it would fill the whole orbit of the moon, and extend 180,000 miles beyond it in all directions.

The sun turns on its axis from west to east; its revolution is performed in about twenty-five days and eight hours. And the sun, attended by its planets, moves in space, at the rate of eight miles every second, in a circular path around a centre, far off in the fields of space; so vast is this path that it will take the sun and the planets which revolve around it, 18,200,000 years to get once completely around that circle. Then the earth is moving with the sun eight miles every second. The first and second heaven is moving with it. Is this not proof that the third heaven must be all around this solar system, and is moving with it in space the same as the first heaven is moving with the earth around the sun? We know we must have the air around the earth so we do not see it move or receive any harm by the earth's rapid movement in space. So I would think that the solar system must have something created all around it, called a third heaven, to protect it, and it is a part of the system and will move with it in space forever; and as we have a number of planets revolving around our sun, so we may suppose there are other suns, with the planets that attend them, following us in the same never-ending path in space. The North Star must be a sun for one of those systems, and if it is following us at the same rate of speed, that would account for its remaining in the same position when viewed from this earth, making a safe and never-changing guide for all who live on this earth.

If all created matter in space is moving, then paradise, or Christ's kingdom, would not remain in one place. And if it was not moving in space with the earth, that part of heaven and earth would, from the creation of man to this time, be a long way apart. And the angels could not ascend and descend from heaven to earth, as we are told they do and have been doing from the creation of man to the present time, and will do it forever. And the air is moving with the earth around the sun, at the rate of more than one thousand miles a minute. This is another proof that the third heaven is moving in space with this solar system. The earth is about

92,000,000 miles from the sun, and Neptune is about 2,746,271,000 miles from the sun, and revolves around it, and that is the farthest planet in this system from the sun. The Bible tells us it is down from heaven to the earth, and it would be down from heaven to the sun, for it is the centre of attraction of this system.

And we go up when we leave any planet that has power to attract, and when we go beyond the reach of that attraction we must go up to the third heaven. Jesus said, after he had been to the third heaven and returned to the earth, he had not ascended to his Father. It would not seem to be proper for the throne of God, the Father, the creator and controller of all created matter in unbounded space, to be in this system of worlds, or in any of the unknown number of systems, like this, that are moving with it in space.

His throne is above all' heavens, or the three heavens spoken of in this system and we are told, "It is he that sitteth upon the circle of the earth." (Isa. 40 : 22.) From this we learn that all planets are round, and all heavens are circles around planets, and around systems of planets. And it takes some planets in this system longer to go around the sun than it does others, because they are farther from it. And there must be systems, with suns and planets attending them, moving around the same field of space we are. Some may be nearer to what we may call the centre of that part of space, and many systems may be moving around the same part of space farther from the centre; as the path of the planet Neptune in this system is 12,654,271,000 miles farther from the sun, or farther from the centre of this system than our earth is. And if the third heaven is around the solar system, there may be a heaven, or something created in empty space, around all systems, or all created matter moving in space. We are told that the "Lord alone hast made heaven, the heaven of heavens." (Neh. 11 : 6.)

Some may think this thought takes us so far off in space it is of no interest to us. Our astronomers do not think so, for they are doing all they can to increase their knowledge of all created matter, and all space around us. It is all right for us to learn all we can about the wonderful works of the Creator, and it is our duty to know, and believe, all he has revealed to us in his Word about our present and our future home, and we should know about the evil spirit who has and will try to hide the truth from us, for he knows we are to be judged by the Word of God. The third heaven would be space that would not be disturbed by planets revolving in it, and could be beyond the reach of the attraction of any of the planets in this system.

No human being could live if they were forced through the air as fast as the earth is moving around the sun, or as fast as this system of planets is moving in space. This is another proof that the space between the sun and the third heaven has nothing

THE LOCATION OF THREE HEAVENS. 23

created in it except the sun and planets; and the unbounded fields of space in which this and other systems are moving is the same. If the sun could, by the law of attraction, hold the farthest planet from it in its place, as it revolves around it, its power of attraction would be strong enough to draw some of the planets to the sun, so I think there is something created in the third heaven around this system of planets to keep them in their proper place; so the flight of the system does not interfere with the planets revolving around the sun. Then the third heaven would be united to this system, as the air is to the earth.

"And he dreamed, and behold, a ladder set up on the earth, and the top of it reached to heaven; and behold the angels of God ascending and descending on it." (Gen. 28 : 12.) From this we learn that heaven is above the earth, and it must be all around it or it could not be above it all the time, and the angels could not be coming down from heaven and return up to heaven, if it was not united to and moving with this solar system.

"And when the Lord came to burn Sodom he said, I will go *down* now and see what they have done." (Gen. 18 : 21.) Down to the earth from the third heaven, and then it would be down to the sun, for that is in the centre of this solar system, and the end of " down " in this system.

All the planets in this system have power to attract to their centres, and that is the end of *down* to each planet; and it is the earth's power to attract to its centre that which holds the air to it and keeps it moving in space with it. The Bible and our astronomers agree as to what is meant by the words "up" and "down," and I think all men should understand the meaning of those words and agree on that point.

And when we think of heaven we should remember that a spiritual body is not like our earthly body. Let us see what the Bible tells us about the angels who have come to the earth and appeared to men in a spiritual body. That will help us understand what kind of a place heaven should be, for them to enjoy it. "When Jesus was transfigured before them, his face did shine as the sun, and his raiment was white as the light." (Matt. 17 : 2.) "And, behold, there was a great earthquake; for the angel of the Lord descended from heaven, and came and rolled back the stone from the door and sat upon it. His countenance was like lightning, and his raiment white as snow." (Matt. 28 : 2, 3.) "The Lord opened the eyes of Balaam, and he saw the angel of the Lord standing in the way, and his sword drawn in his hand." (Num. 22 : 31.) The angel had been before Balaam some time and he could not see him; this proves that a spiritual body could stand before us and we could not see it. "And Elisha prayed, and said, Lord, I pray thee, open his eyes, that he may see. And the Lord opened the eyes of the young man and he saw, and behold! the mountain was full of horses and chariots of fire round about

Elisha." (2 Kings 6:17.) When Jesus appeared to Saul, who was Paul, "he saw a light from heaven." (Acts 9:3.) That light was Jesus, and he spoke to Saul.

And as the Lord can change a natural body to a spiritual body, so he can change a spiritual body to what appears to be a natural body.

For Jesus and his angels appeared to men on the earth in a body that looked like a human body. It was in the form of men that the Lord and his two angels appeared to Abraham. (Gen. 18:2.)

And angels have often appeared on the earth in the form of men. But the spiritual body is the body they have in heaven. And that spiritual body could not be confined. It can pass through space called heaven, or through the rock-bound walls of earth. The third heaven could be made a suitable home for the angels and the redeemed, as the air is for the human body to sustain life. Some may say the angels could live on some of the planets in this solar system. They could; but the Lord has not called any of the planets heaven. And he has told us there is a heaven, and he calls it the third heaven, paradise, and Christ's kingdom. It is the home of Abraham, Isaac, and Jacob. And Christ has told us they are alive in heaven, and not dead; for God is the God of the living and not of the dead. For the Lord created man a living soul, and his spirit will never die. And if all the redeemed in the past, and all in the future to the end of time, go to the third heaven and return to the earth with the Son of God at his last coming, the third heaven they live in must have moved in space with this system of planets, or it would not be above the earth, as the Bible tells us it is; and if it did not move it would be a long way from the earth now, and farther yet at the end of time. I do not see what reason we can give for refusing to believe what the Bible tells us about the location of the third heaven.

We can find no place more suitable for Christ's kingdom, for he is preparing his subjects on earth, for heaven, and his kingdom should be above all created matter in this system of planets.

And the throne of God, the Father, should be above all systems he has created, and may be in that part of space, or heaven, around which all the systems of planets, or all he has created, are revolving, and will continue to revolve in perfect order for all eternity, controlled by the unbounded power of the God who created them in unbounded space.

The Creator has given men his spirit to give them wisdom to write the Bible; and he will give *us* his spirit, which will give us wisdom enough to understand it, if we will ask him for it and *believe* he will give it. In that way we honor him, and then he has promised to honor us and take us to his home. "Fear not, little flock; for it is your father's good pleasure to give you the kingdom." (Luke 12 : 32.) This is told us by his only begotten and well-beloved Son, in whom he was well pleased, and he has told us to hear him, and that son has given himself a ransom for us. Men do not understand the Bible, for they allow the devil to blind them, and they believe what men tell them, and do not believe what the Lord has told them in his Word about heaven. Men believe there is a creator, and they believe he has a home somewhere up in space he calls heaven. They believe this because they find it in the Bible, and they believe the God of heaven is the author of the Bible. Then why not believe *all* that the Bible has told us about his home in heaven? He calls all space heaven, and then divides it into three heavens, and the third heaven up from the earth he calls paradise, and Christ's kingdom; and Christ tells us his Father's throne is above that, or above all heavens, meaning the three heavens that must belong to this system of worlds. Why not believe that? for Christ must know where heaven is; and he has not called any of the planets heaven. Then where else could Christ's kingdom be in this system? for the system and all the planets in it are moving in perfect order, and they are moving around a circle. And the Lord calls the heavens he has created a circle, and as the first heaven is a circle around the earth, the third heaven must be a circle around this system of planets moving in space, with the sun for its centre. Then heaven, earth, and hell must move with it in space.

If we should change the meaning of what men tell us, as we do what the Lord has told us about the location of heaven and hell, and the second coming of Christ, they would take it as an insult. It is not enough for us to think we believe and obey it all; for the Jews thought they understood and believed all the prophets had told them as to the Messiah's coming. But they refused to believe on him because he did not accomplish all that was thus declared at his first coming, which he will fulfill at his second coming. And for that mistake the Lord has forsaken and scattered them. We should profit by the mistakes of those who have gone before us. Will the judge of all the earth say we are doing it? He will not, if we are judged by the rule he has judged men by in the past.

I know it is almost impossible for men to change their views as to the teachings of the Bible. The old ruts are inviting, and very few ever leave them. But that does not prove they are the right way; and men have found so many ways they think are right that it may be well for us to hold them up to the light given us in the Word of God, and, when we do it, make our opinions yield to the will and word of God.

WHAT THE BIBLE TELLS US ABOUT THE LOCATION OF HELL.

THIS subject will not interest many of our fallen race, for very few think they will ever go to hell; for nearly all men think they have, or will mark out, some way that will prepare them for heaven. But they do not learn this from the Bible; for Christ has told us we must "Strive to enter in at the strait gate; for many, I say unto you, will seek to enter in, and shall not be able." (Luke 13 : 24.)

"For his spirit shall not always strive with man." (Gen. 6 : 3.) And he said, "Broad is the way that leadeth to destruction, and many there be which go in thereat. Because strait is the gate and narrow is the way which leadeth unto life, and few there be that find it." (Matt. 7 : 13, 14.)

Christ speaks for one in hell, and tells us he wanted one sent from the dead to warn his five brothers, and tell them not to come to that place of torment, for he was tormented in that flame. And Christ told him, if they would not hear Moses and the prophets, they would not hear, though one rose from the dead. Christ would not misrepresent the condition of the lost. From this we learn that the devil will deceive many, and it is the duty of men to know and believe all the Lord has revealed to us in his word on this subject. For if the Lord has thought it worth revealing, we have no right to say it is of no interest to us. For the word of the Lord is given to us to instruct us in this life, and it will be of no use to us in a future state, and we cannot return to warn our fellow-men. For then the harvest is past, and if our soul is not saved it will never be saved. Believing this, and knowing I am not responsible for what is in the Bible on this subject, and believing I have been led by the Holy Spirit to investigate this part of God's Word, and have been taught to understand and believe it, I think I would not discharge a duty I owe to the author of the Bible and to my fellow-men if I did not give them the result of this investigation. "And he that hath my word, let him speak my word faithfully; what is the chaff to the wheat? saith the Lord." (Jer. 23 : 28.) If we do not believe what the Bible tells us about the devil's home and its location, and teach men not to believe it, we are giving them chaff and not the wheat, or the truth of the Bible. The Lord has told us to " Say unto the wicked, Thou shalt surely die; and if we do not warn the wicked man, he shall die in his iniquity; and the Lord will require his blood at our hand. But if we warn the wicked, and he turn not from his wickedness, he shall die in his iniquity; but thou hast delivered thy soul." (Ezek. 3 : 18, 19.)

I deem this a sufficient reason for calling attention to what the Lord has told us in His word about the future home of all who are not saved in heaven.

If all who are living on the earth, but at the end of this life will be lost, could know it now, there would be more interested and willing to know what the author of the Bible has told us on this subject than there is. To prove this point, I will give you a few words the Son of God has said about it.

"Not every one that saith unto me, Lord, Lord, shall enter into the kingdom of heaven: but he that doeth the will of my Father, which is in heaven. Many will say to me in that day, Lord, Lord, have we not prophesied in thy name? and in thy name have cast out devils? and in thy name done many wonderful works? And then will I profess unto them, I never knew you; depart from me, ye that work iniquity." (Matt. 7 : 21, 22, 23.)

"Ye did run well: who did hinder you, that ye should not obey the truth?" (Gal. 5 : 7.) Again, Paul said, "I keep under my body, and bring it into subjection; lest that by any means, when I have preached to others, I myself should be a castaway." (1 Cor. 9 : 27.) And again, Christ tells the Jews they have killed the prophets, and stoned them which are sent unto them; "how often would I have gathered thy children together, even as a hen gathereth her chickens under her wings, and ye *would not*." (Matt. 23 : 37.) The Jews were all willing to be saved, and believed they would be taken to heaven, for they had Abraham for their Father. But they wanted to work out their salvation in their own way, and they did not want any one to oppose them, or to tell them they must go some other way to find heaven, and that they must trust in Christ, and give their personal obedience to Him, and not rely on what had been done by Abraham in his day. The devil is persuading many to take the same view of salvation in our day. They want to go to heaven on a road that is broad enough to let all men in, if they have a roll of self-righteousness under one arm and a roll of self-will under the other. Christ has told us if we would be his disciples "we must take up *our* cross," not ask some one else to do it, and then we must "follow him"—not follow Abraham, or some one who has no power to save us; for Christ is the way, and the only one who has the power to save us from the effects of the fall. I think this gives us reason to fear that many of our fellow-men will never be permitted to ascend to heaven. Then is it not our duty to tell them what is revealed to us in the Word of God about the home of the lost, as much as it is to tell them about heaven, the home of the saved? It is in Christ's gospel, and that must be preached to all nations. But some tell us that all the Bible has in it about the home of the lost is not to be understood by the meaning of the words used. I find nothing in the Bible to build a theory of that kind on. If those who believe that the Bible is a divine revelation take the liberty to change that part of God's Word, how can we prevent those who do not want to believe it as it is, if they want to change some other part of the Word of God? Satan does not want men to believe what the Bible has told us about *his* home. Is it the power the evil spirit has over men that has prevented them from believing what the Bible says as to the location and the description given of the devil's abode? If that is the case, it is time his power and control over men as to that part of God's Word is broken, and that those who preach the gospel should be at liberty to declare the whole counsel of God.

The Word of God tells that the heavens are above and around the earth, and Satan's place is down from heaven to the earth, and then down below, or under the earth we live on, and that it is in a lake of fire (and we have a lake of fire in the earth). Some may say this could not be. "Is anything too hard for the Lord?" He protected men in a furnace of fire, and in the lions' den; and we do not know what the soul or spirit of man can endure, for we have never seen it, but the Creator of all things has seen it. Some may refuse to believe it because it has been concealed so long from men who have believed the Bible; that does not prove it is not true if it is in the Bible. I will, therefore, as a duty try to explain what I understand is revealed in the Word of God about the location and the description given us of the place he has prepared for the residence of the devil and his angels, and all who are not saved from the wrath to come—or those who are not God's children.

I wish to say to all who read this book, If you want to understand God's Word, you must believe what you find in it. The Jews refused to believe what the prophets told them, and what Christ told them, but that did not change the truths of revelation; and if we refuse to believe what is taught us in the Word of God on this subject, that will not change the location of the devil's home, or take men to heaven.

If the Creator has thought best to reveal so much to us on this subject, is it wisdom for men who attempt to explain the Bible to their fellow-men to tell them not to believe it? I think it is not. "For this truth and prophecy came not in old time by the will of man, but holy men of God spake as they were moved by the Holy Ghost." (2 Pet. 1 : 21.) If we believe what the Bible has told us about the third heaven surrounding this system of worlds, with the sun for its centre and lowest point, that will help us to understand what the Lord means when he speaks of coming down from heaven to the earth, and from the earth down into hell. And the Bible has been written to instruct men who live on the earth; and the Word of God tells us we must go down, not up, or away from this earth, to find the home he has prepared for the devil. All that is said on this subject may be classed with prophecy, and we are told that prophecy has no private interpretation; and we should be guided by the meaning of the words used by the prophets to convey truth to us on this subject. Christ said he " beheld Satan as lightning fall from heaven."

(Luke 10 : 18.) We understand that we go down when we fall, and the devil must have come down to the earth when he was driven from heaven.

The first account we have of his work on the earth was in the Garden of Eden. When he told Eve to eat the forbidden fruit, and said to her, "Ye shall not surely die" (Gen. 3 : 4); that was a lie and he has been deceiving men in the same way from that time to this. We find him on the earth when man was created; and we can prove by his works with men that he and his angels have been on the earth from that time to the present, and we are told that an angel will come down from heaven to the earth, to chain and shut up the devil and Satan, and seal up the prison for a thousand years, so he cannot deceive the nations any more till the thousand years are ended; and at the end of that time the devil will be loosed from his prison, and the Lord will permit him to deceive men who will live on the earth then. The angel came to the earth, the devil's home, to confine him in prison, he does not say he took him to some other planet to confine him, and this prison, called a bottomless pit, could not be in open space, called heaven, and when he is loosed from his prison to deceive men there is nothing said about bringing him to the earth; but we are told that he is on the earth and men engage in war; the spear which had been turned to a pruning-hook is then made into a spear, and is used to kill men; this is Satan's work. When the devil and all his, at the end of the age of man, are to be confined for ever in a lake of fire, there is nothing said then, about taking him and the lost of Adam's race from the earth. "And if God spared not the angels that sinned, but cast them down to hell, and delivered them into chains of darkness, to be reserved unto judgment." (2 Pet. 2 : 4.) They were cast down to the earth, and will be kept here till the end of the race of Adam; and then the devil, and all who are his, will be confined forever in the lake of fire in this earth. It is a prison, and is called a bottomless pit, in which they are all to be confined for ever, and that prison is called a lake of fire that will burn for ever. We have all that in this earth, and if some other planet in this system has a lake of fire in it, we would have to leave this earth and go up through the air called heaven to find it, and we have no orders in the Bible to go up, or leave this earth, to find hell, or the devil's home; and at the end of the age of man Christ will come with his elect and surround the earth, and all his children living on the earth then will be caught up with him, and changed from a natural to a spiritual body; and those who are not his will be left on the earth; then the unrighteous dead are raised, and they must come from the earth; and they do not leave it, for we are told they "will say to the mountains and rocks, Fall on us, and hide us from the face of him that sitteth on the throne, and from the wrath of the Lamb. For the great day of his wrath is come, and who shall be able to stand?" (Rev. 6 : 16, 17.) "And the sea gave up the dead which were in it; and death and hell delivered up the dead which were in them; and they were judged every man according to their works; and death and hell were cast into the lake of fire. This is the second death, and whosoever was not found written in the book of life was cast into the lake of fire." (Rev. 20 : 13, 14, 15.). Not UP TO, but INTO, the lake of fire.

This will be done at the third and last coming of Christ, to burn the air, melt the hills, and make all things new. And to confine the devil and the lost in the lake of fire that is in this earth; a fire that was kindled in this earth long before man was created. For the Lord has said, "A fire is kindled in mine anger, and shall burn unto the lowest hell, and shall consume the earth with her increase, and set on fire the foundations of the mountains." (Deut. 32: 22.) The foundations of the mountains confine the lake of fire which is in this earth. And at the end of the world it will burn up all the works of man called the increase of the earth. And that fire is to burn to the lowest hell, or the centre of this earth, for that is the end of down, or the lowest place in this earth. "Though they dig into hell, thence shall mine hand take them; though they climb up to heaven, thence will I bring them down." (Amos 9:2.)

I have shown now that all the redeemed are taken up to heaven, and will return to the earth with Christ at his last coming. And all the lost, who have, by their works on the earth, at the end of this life been left with the god of this world, will after the last resurrection be ordered to return to the same place of torment. "Hell is naked before him, and destruction hath no covering" (to conceal it from the Creator). "He stretcheth out the north over the empty place, and hangeth the earth upon nothing." (Job 26:6, 7.) Job understood, then, that the earth was hung on nothing. What empty place does he refer to? Was it the lake of fire in this earth that would be most empty at that time if it was compared to what it will be at the end of the world?

The devil makes most men believe that hell is not a lake of fire, and it is not in this earth. That is nothing new for him, for he makes men believe a lie is the truth when ever he can. Men in all ages of the world have believed there was a place of reward and punishment in a future state. And if men who attempt to explain the Bible tell us they do not know where hell is, or what kind of a place it is, leaving all those who look to them for instruction in darkness on this subject, withholding from them the light the Lord has given to us in his Word, the result will be that all who want instruction on this subject will come to this conclusion, that if the preacher does not understand what is said in the Bible about hell, and its location, they will not try to understand or believe what is said about it. They are then left to form all kinds of opinions about hell, and very few would think alike on this subject; for every one would be left to form his own opinion. This is a mistake, for the author of the Bible does not intend for us to be left in the dark about the future home of the lost. And I do not think the Lord will be pleased with men he has called to explain his Word, if they do not understand, believe, and explain what he has revealed to them in that Word on this subject.

All that men have said or written about hell amounts to nothing if it is not founded on the Bible. If the Lord has told us where it is located, and what kind of a place it is, then all men should believe it; for the Lord has revealed it. He has told us heaven, or Christ's kingdom, is up in the third heave-up from the earth; all are willing to believe heaven is up. The Lord has told all men who live on the earth that hell is down. That is the opposite to up. It is all plain; we understand the meaning of the word down as well as we do the word up. The meaning of heaven is, heave-up. And hell means a covered or concealed place. The lake of fire in this earth would be a prison that would cover and conceal the lost from the light of heaven. The word down derives its meaning from the law of attraction, and this earth attracts to its centre; that is the end of down so far as this world is concerned. The sun is the centre of this system of worlds and attracts to its centre. But that attraction does not interfere with or control the earth's attraction. Then if men on all sides of this earth are ordered to go down, they must go down to the centre of this earth, and say that is the end of down, for they would weigh nothing at that point, for the earth could not attract there. The interior of this earth can be called a lake of fire, and it could be called a bottomless pit, for there would be no bottom or foundation at the centre. And the foundation of the mountains are all outside, and forms the prison walls to confine the lake of fire and brimstone in this earth. "And thou, Capernaum, which art exalted unto heaven, shalt be brought *down* to hell, for if the mighty works which have been done in thee had been done in Sodom, it would have remained until this day." (Matt. 11 : 23.)

God's truth has been made plainer to us; do we understand and believe it? If Christ should ask us why we do not believe we must go down to find hell, what reason could we give for wanting to go up from this earth in space called heaven, to some other planet in this system, and then go down in that to find the devil's place of confinement? And if it did not correspond with the interior of this earth we could not say it was the home for the lost described in the Bible. And it could not be in open space, for it must be surrounded by prison walls, so that the Lord could seal it up for a thousand years and then open it, and loose the devil from his prison. "And I saw a star fall from heaven unto the earth; and to him was given the key of the bottomless pit. And he opened the bottomless pit, and there arose a smoke out of the pit, as the smoke of a great furnace; and the sun and the air were darkened by reason of the smoke of the pit, and there came out of the smoke locusts upon the earth; and unto them was given power, as the scorpions of the earth have power. And it was commanded them that they should not hurt the grass of the earth, neither any green thing, neither any tree; but only those men which have not the seal of God in their foreheads. And to them it was given that they should not kill them, but that they should be tormented five months: and their torment was as the torment of a scorpion when he striketh a man. And in those days shall men seek death, and shall not find it; and shall desire to die, and death shall flee from them. And the shape of the locusts were like unto horses prepared unto battle; and on their heads were as it were crowns like gold, and their faces were as the faces of men. And they had hair as the hair of women; and their teeth were as the teeth of lions. And they had breastplates as it were of iron; and the sound of their wings was as the sound of chariots, of many horses running to battle. And they had tails like unto scorpions, and there were stings in their tails; and their power was to hurt men five months. And they had a king over them which is the angel of the bottomless pit." (Rev. 9 : 1-11.)

This prophecy has not been fulfilled yet, but it will be, on this earth, before the end comes. The prophet Joel in the second chapter, tells us of the same event more than 800 years before John wrote this in Revelation. Please read the second chapter of Joel and compare it. I think no one can deny or change the statements made by the prophets, that the bottomless pit, opened then, was opened on this earth. The leader of the fallen angels, with his host, came out of the opening made by the star that fell from heaven to the earth. And the Lord permits them to do this to torment men on this earth for their wickedness, but they are not allowed to kill them, and they will not harm God's children who live on the earth at that time. This all goes to show that it will be while the devil is permitted to deceive men. And good and bad men will live on the earth then as now. The time they torment men is five months, and it must be done before the end of the world, for men are in human form, and good and evil is on the earth. When a preacher is talking about hell, he points down, but does not tell what he means by it. If he could go in the direction he pointed till he could meet a preacher from the other side of the earth, they could then say they had found the end of down, and it was in the centre of this earth. As right is the opposite to wrong, so heaven is the opposite to hell. If a man is told to climb up in a tree, and one to go down in a well, they would both understand what you told them. But when God tells us we must climb up to heaven, and go down, or dig into hell, men do not understand him. If we look at this, and think it over, we will see the devil is blinding men, and concealing this truth from them. They should tell him to get behind them, and then they can understand and believe this part of God's word.

At Christ's last coming to the earth to make all things new, he brings his elect with him. But he has said nothing about bringing the devil and the souls of the lost to the earth. And he has not told us in the Bible they will ever be taken from the earth or return to it. They will be on the earth, and in it, and when they are taken out of hell to judgment, will want the mountains to hide them from the Son of God. They did not love him when they lived on the earth, and they will not love him then. For they know he will tell them to depart from him into everlasting fire, prepared for the devil and his angels. The devil is called a deceiver, and all men should see that he does not deceive them, or make them believe hell is up from the earth in space, when the Bible tells us it is down in the earth. If the Lord had not intended for us to make some use of what he has said about hell, he would not have said so much about it. If men who profess to believe the Bible is a divine revelation do not understand or believe what the Bible tells them about hell, can they blame those who do not believe the Bible if they say there is no hell, and make no effort to escape from it, or try to secure eternal life? For they know nothing about eternal death, or eternal separation from the God of Heaven. I think it is our duty to believe all the Son of God and the Holy Spirit have told us about heaven and hell, or the unseen worlds. It will do us no harm, and it may do others good, and show our respect for the author of the Bible by believing what he has revealed to us. "And then shall he send his angels, and shall gather together his elect from the four winds, from the uttermost part of the earth, to the uttermost part of heaven." (Mark 13 : 27.) That includes all heaven and all the earth, but not hell or the lost.

All space is called heaven, and hell must be in this earth or in some other planet in this system of worlds, for no other place is found. "Who shall ascend into heaven to bring Christ down from above? or who shall descend into the deep, to bring up Christ again from the dead?" (Rom. 10 : 6.) That calls the grave deep; hell is in the same direction, only deeper; and the sea is called deep. "The Lord looked down from heaven upon the children of men, to see if any did understand God." (Psa. 14 : 2.) This is very plain, and all could understand Him if they could understand what up and down means, for it is very plain in the Bible. The devil wants men to add to or take from the Word of God. And he does not want us to believe hell, or his home, is in this earth. The Son of God was a plain preacher on this subject, and if it was not the truth, the devil would have told Christ, when he tempted him, that what He had said about his home, and what was said about it in the Bible, was not true. "To go into hell, into the fire that never shall be quenched . . . where their worm dieth not, and the fire is not quenched. To be cast into hell, into the fire that never shall be quenched . . . where their worm dieth not, and the fire is not quenched. To be cast into hell fire . . . where their worm dieth not, and the fire is not quenched." This is the language used by the Son of God, and recorded in Mark 9 : 43, 48.

What do men do with this when they say they do not believe hell is a lake of fire? " The wicked shall be turned into hell, and all the nations that forget God." (Psa. 9 : 17.) This does not refer to the body in the grave, but to the soul in the fire of hell; and they are not carried away to hell, but turned into hell! The word bottomless pit is in the Book of Revelation seven times, and it refers to the devil's home, and locates it in this earth. " The beast that ascendeth out of the bottomless pit shall make war against them and kill them." (Rev. 11 : 7.) This beast, or the devil, did not come down to the earth to make war with men, but he ascended or came up out of the bottomless pit that is in the earth. "The beast shall ascend out of the bottomless pit, and they that dwell on the earth shall wonder." (Rev. 17 : 8.) "Nor height, nor depth, nor any other creature, shall be able to separate us from the love of God." (Rom. 8 : 39.) Christ "was set up from everlasting, from the beginning, or ever the earth was. When there were no depths, I was brought forth. Before the mountains were settled, before the hills, was I brought forth." (Prov. 8 : 23, 24, 25.) In this the Son of God would have us understand he was with his Father before the world was, or before there were any depths or mountains. There are depths in this earth that would interest men on the earth, the creation of which he was talking about. Christ ordered the legion of devils out of the man; "and the devils besought him that he would not command them to go into the deep." (Luke 8 : 31.) They did not want to go down in the lake of fire in this earth, called deep. They wanted to go in the swine, and drive them into the sea, and then enter into the men who lived in that place, and make them believe that Christ was the person who made the swine go into the sea; and the devils got the men to pray for Christ "to depart out of their coast."

The devil is doing the same kind of work now. "And Balaam answered and said unto the servants of Balak: If Balak would give me his house full of silver and gold, I cannot go beyond the word of the Lord my God, to do less or more." (Num. 22 : 18.) If that prophet could not change the word of the Lord in a case as trifling as that, can we think the Son of God and, all the prophets who point to the location of hell, and give the same description of it, could do so if it was not true, and did not correspond with what had been revealed to them by the God of heaven? "And when Balaam went with the princes of Moab, the Lord sent his angel to stop him, and when the ass saw the angel of the Lord she fell down under Balaam. And the Lord opened the mouth of the ass, and she said unto Balaam, What have I done unto thee, that thou hast smitten me these three times? Then the Lord opened the eyes of Balaam, and he saw the angel of the Lord standing in the way and his sword drawn in his hand; and he bowed down his head and fell flat on his face. And Balaam said unto the angel of the Lord, I have sinned." (Num. 22 : 21, 28, 31, 34.) That prophet did not change the word of the Lord, and the Lord sent a prophet from Judah to Bethel to tell Jeroboam about the birth of Christ: "Behold, a child shall be born unto the house of David, Josiah by name." And the king wanted the man of God to come in and refresh himself, and he would give him a reward. The man of God said he would not go in and eat bread with him for half his house, for the Lord told him not to eat bread or drink water in that place, and not to return by the way he went. So he went another way, and returned not by the way he came. And the devil sent a prophet after him, and he wanted the man of God to come home with him and eat bread, and the prophet refused to go; but the devil's prophet lied to him, and told him an angel of the Lord had told him that he, the the man of God, could go back and eat bread with him. So he went back with him and did eat bread in his house; he disobeyed, and it cost him his life. And the Lord told him, for disobeying his command, his carcass should not come to the sepulchre of his fathers, and on his way home a lion met him by the way and slew him. (1 Kings 13.)

I refer to these historic events recorded in the Bible to show the readers of this book that it was not safe for a prophet of the Lord, at that time, to change the word of the Lord, or try to do it. Is it safe for men in this age of the world to change the meaning of the words used by the inspired writers to explain God's truth to us, and tell men that this and that part of his Word is not to be understood, or obeyed as it is written? Men in all ages of the world have been doing more or less of this, and in many cases the inspired writers have given us an account of how the Lord dealt with men who changed some of his small commands, and did something they thought would do as well. We must remember, if the Lord has told us to do or believe something, and we are tempted to do something that would take the place of it, or do as well as the Lord's command *in our estimation*, the evil spirit is the author of that change, and we are told, "For I testify unto every man that heareth the words of the prophecy of this book, If any man shall add unto these things, God shall add unto him the plagues that are written in this book." (Rev. 22: 18.) The same if we take from it. "The words of the Lord are pure words, as silver tried in a furnace of earth, purified seven times." (Psa. 12:6.) The Lord has given us his Word, and he has a right to tell us it is pure as silver can be, and is composed of truth unmixed with error, and will all be fulfilled; and we have no right to change it. If we take this view of that part of God's Word which describes and locates hell, how can we change it, or refuse to believe what the Lord has said about it, and say we love, believe, and want to obey the author of the Bible? I will leave this for the reader to answer. The prophet has told us that "By these three was the third part of men killed: by the fire, and by the smoke, and by the brimstone, which issued out of their mouths; and the rest of the men that were not killed by these plagues repented not, but worshiped devils and idols." (Rev. 9 : 18, 20.) The evil spirits with the leader of the fallen angels will come out of the earth and do this after the devil's release from prison. And the other two-thirds worshipped devils and idols, and would not repent. "Then shall he say also unto them on his left hand, Depart from me, ye cursed, into everlasting fire prepared for the devil and his angels." (Matt. 25 : 41.) At that time, the Son of God, with all whom he calls his children, are in the air around the earth with those who had been caught up and changed in the twinkling of an eye. He does not tell the lost to go in space above him, but they are to go into everlasting fire. We have fire in this earth; can we find another? and to find it we will not go *up*.

The devil is called "the prince of this world" (John 12 : 31) and "the God of this world." (2 Cor.

4 : 4) He is a god and ruler over all men who are not delivered from his power and control by the Son of God. Christ is called the light of the world : and the devil uses all the power he has over the minds of men to conceal that light, called wisdom, that cometh down from above. We are told by that light to try the spirit that is trying to control or instruct us, that is, by the light of God's Word, before we decide to obey and be governed by it.

The Bible gives us all the instruction we want in this life. And it throws a light on the unseen worlds, if we do not allow the devil to throw his dark mantle over it. We are told that " Jesus was full of the Holy Ghost when He was tempted forty days by the devil. And in those days He did eat nothing." (Luke 4 : 2.) Christ could have turned the stones into bread, for he did create bread after that, and turn water into wine. But if he had done it when the devil told him to do it, he would have obeyed him, and that would have made him the devil's servant, and he could not have been offered as a sinless sacrifice for us. There was no harm in Christ turning the stones to bread, if the devil had not asked him to do it. The devil tells men to do and believe many things now, and men do not see any harm in it, and there would be no harm or sin in it if the devil had not told them to do it, or believe him instead of the Word of God. By that we know and should believe its author. If we do not believe hell is a lake of fire down in a bottomless pit in this earth, a covered and concealed place, called a prison, in which the devil, his angels and the souls of all the lost are to be confined forever—where the soul dieth not and the fire is not quenched forever (a truth that is made very plain in the Bible), is it not the devil who tells us not to believe that part of God's Word ? It was the devil who would not let the Jews believe that Christ was to come and be offered a sacrifice for sin before he would be a king on the throne of David. And the same evil spirit prevents men, now, from believing Christ will come, and confine the devil, bring salvation to all who live on the earth for a thousand years, and then loose him to deceive the nations of the earth before the end comes.

The history of the Jews from that time to the present proves that they believed and obeyed the devil, and not the prophets, or the instruction given to them in the Word of God. And if it has not benefited them to be governed by and to obey the devil, it will not pay us or any of our race. "For the grave cannot praise thee; death cannot celebrate thee; they that go down into the pit cannot hope for thy truth." (Isaiah 38 : 18.) All who go to the grave without receiving the pardon offered them in the Bible will go down into the pit called hell, and will receive no benefit from God's truth. The body in the grave, or the soul in hell, will not praise him if they go DOWN into the pit. But all who go UP to heaven will praise him. "For as the heavens are higher than the earth, so are my ways higher than your ways, and my thoughts than your thoughts, saith the Lord." (Isaiah 55 : 9.) That locates heaven above and around the earth. "But will God indeed dwell on the earth? Behold, the heaven and heaven of heavens cannot contain thee." (1 Kings 8 : 27.) "Thus saith the Lord, If heaven above can be measured, and the foundations of the earth searched out beneath." (Jer. 31 : 37.) "The heaven for height and the earth for depth." (Prov. 25 : 3.) "Her house is the way to hell, going DOWN to the chambers of death." (Prov. 7 : 27.)

In this we are told the lost go DOWN when they go to hell—called eternal death—and not UP or away from the earth. The redeemed will go down to the grave, but their souls will leave the earth and ascend to heaven, to eternal life, or eternal union with the God of heaven, and be free from the god of this world. "Thus saith the Lord God, In the day when he went down to the grave, I made the nations to shake at the sound of his fall; when I cast him down to hell with them that descend into the pit, they also went down into hell." (Ezek. 31 : 15, 16, 17.) "Son of man, wail for the multitude of Egypt, and cast them down, her and the daughters of the famous nations, into the nether parts of the earth, with them that go down into the pit. . . . The strong among the mighty shall speak to him out of the midst of hell; with them that help him they are gone down; they lie uncircumcised, slain by the sword. Asshur is there, and all her company; his graves are about him, all of them slain, fallen by the sword," or death. (Ezek. 32 : 18, 21, 22.) "Whose graves are set in the sides of the pit, and her company is round about her grave, all of them slain, fallen by the sword, which caused terror in the land of the living." (Ezek. 32 : 23.) The prophet speaks of men who have lived on the earth, or in the land of the living, but had been slain by the sword of death, and their graves are in the sides of the pit. Friends living on the earth are round about their graves, and their souls had gone down into hell, and they were to wail for the multitude of Egypt. That must refer to the multitude who were drowned in the Red Sea. Their bodies were in the sea, but their souls had gone down into the nether parts of the earth, with them who go down to the pit. Hell is called a pit, and I do not see how we can be mistaken about the location of the pit pointed to by the prophet as the eternal home of the souls of the host of Egypt. The multitude of Elam, and the company of Asshur, with those who had been strong and mighty on the earth, but now must speak to him out of the midst of hell, they were not on the earth then, for they had been slain by the sword of death. We are not told that angels took them to any other place in space, or took them from the earth, but they were taken down into the pit. "There is Edom; her kings and all her princes have gone down to the pit. There be the princes of the north, all of them bear their shame with them that go down to the pit. Pharaoh shall see them, and shall be comforted over all his multitude; even Pharaoh and all his army slain by the sword, saith the Lord." (Ezek. 32 : 29, 30, 31.) Pharaoh and his army had been drowned nine hundred years before the Lord ordered Ezekiel to write this. The Lord knew where Pharaoh and his army were, and where he was sending the souls of all those the prophet speaks of. And he knew that Pharaoh was glad to see the Jews come to that place of torment with him and his host. "And the earth opened her mouth and swallowed up Korah and his company; and they all went down alive into the pit, and the earth closed upon them." (Num. 16 : 32, 33.) Did the souls of that company who went down with their bodies in the earth go on down when they left the body to the lake of fire and bottomless pit in the earth, or did they come up from that pit and go on up in space to find the home of the evil spirit who had advised them not to be ruled over by Moses, and who refused to obey the Lord who had delivered them from Egypt? He had done for them many wonderful works, that should have convinced them that they had not been delivered by the hand of Moses, but by the Lord, who ruled the earth, and had control of all created things. The result of that rebellion, and lessons of that kind, recorded in the Bible, should warn us not to try experiments, or even refuse to believe what is revealed, or refuse to obey the commands the Lord has given us in his Word. They went down in the earth in the pit, and the earth swallowed them up. If the soul or spirit (which is the person) came up from that pit and then went up from the earth in space to find the home of that evil spirit, and the home the Lord has prepared for him and all the lost, I think the Lord would have told us about it; for the inspired writers have been careful to give a correct account of all that was done by men, right or wrong.

All that the Lord has said to us in the Bible about heaven tells us it is up in space from the earth. And all they have said about the home of the fallen angels locates it on this earth; and their future home, in which they are to be confined forever, is in the earth. " And he lifted up his eyes, being in torment, and seeth Abraham afar off and Lazarus in his bosom. And he cried and said, Father Abraham, have mercy on me, and send Lazarus that he may dip the tip of his finger in water and cool my tongue, for I am tormented in this flame." (Luke 16 : 23, 24.) What right have we to say the description given by the Son of God of the rich man in hell does not give a true picture of hell and all the lost? He selects a man who had not been in hell long, and a man who supposed himself prepared for heaven; and his brothers on the earth supposed he was, for they were living in the same way. He calls Abraham his father. He had five brothers living on the earth, and he did not want them to come to that place of torment: and he wanted one sent from the dead to tell them not to come to that place. And Christ said if they would not believe what Moses and the prophets had said to them, they would not believe if one went from the dead. Christ raised himself and others from the dead, and many who lived in his day did not believe on him. Christ tells us he could see into heaven. We do not know how far the spiritual eye of the lost can see, and there are openings in the earth for the lake of fire, and the prison walls are not sealed up yet. And Stephen said he could see the Son of God in heaven before his death, and the lost could see from this earth to heaven as well as they could from any other planet in this system of worlds.

The Lord told Saul to " go and smite Amalek, and spare nothing." Saul went, and took a large army with him, and could have done all the Lord had told him to do. He destroyed all the people except the king, and took him to Samuel. And he spared the best sheep, lambs, and oxen. He spared them to make a sacrifice unto the Lord. And then Samuel told him that to obey was better than sacrifice, and rebellion was as the sin of witchcraft, and because he had rejected the word of the Lord he would be rejected by the Lord from being king. And then Saul said, the people took the sheep and oxen; but the Lord held Saul responsible, for he could have controlled the people. " And Samuel came no more to see Saul until the day of his death." (1 Sam. 15.) Twenty-four years from this event the Philistines gathered themselves together to make war on Saul, and when Saul saw the host he was afraid. And

Saul inquired of the Lord, and he answered him not. And the evil spirit that had controlled Saul advised him to go and see a witch; and Saul disguised himself, and put on other raiment, and went as directed. (1 Sam. 28.) Saul knew how to inquire of the Lord, and said he could not receive any answer. Then, the Lord did not send him to the witch, but he went to see her as led to do by the devil. The woman was afraid to grant his request. For Saul had put the witches and wizards to death, and she thought some one was laying a snare for her life. And Saul swore by the Lord that she should not be harmed. Then she asked, " Whom shall I bring up unto thee?" And he said, " Bring up Samuel," for the evil spirit never wanted his servants to call for him, as he could deceive them better under the mantle of some one the person wanted to see. The person or spirit who came up at her call told her she was talking to King Saul, and she cried with a loud voice and asked Saul why he had deceived her. And the king said unto her, " Be not afraid, for what sawest thou? And the woman said unto Saul, I saw gods ascending out of the earth. And he said unto her, What form is he of? And she said, An old man cometh up and he is covered with a mantle." Saul had deceived the woman, and now the devil had deceived him, for he thought it was Samuel. He would not have come from heaven and said to Saul, " Why hast thou disquieted me, to bring me up?" Think of Samuel coming up out of the ground, at the call of a witch, and then finding fault because he had to come and see a witch whom he would not have spoken to when he was living on the earth! If Samuel had come as described, Saul could have seen him if the woman could. Satan knew that Saul had nothing left to rely on but his courage, and he wanted to take that from him. And he did it by telling him what he claimed Samuel had told him through the witch. And Saul fell on the earth, and was sore afraid. Think of the King of Israel on the ground in a stable! for the woman had a fat calf in the house, and she killed it, and perhaps Saul ate his last meal in that hut with a witch, and food prepared by her for them. They did not ask Satan, whom they had called to bring up Samuel to dine with them. But that spirit had done his work well. For Saul was not fit then to be a king or the commander of an army. He would not believe what Samuel had told him in his lifetime, but he believed what he supposed Samuel had told him when he came from heaven at the call of a witch. The following is what the Lord told the Jews to do with a witch. "Thou shalt not suffer a witch to live." (Ex. 22:18.) "There shall not be among you a witch." (Deut. 18:10.) "The soul that turns after wizards I will cut off." (Lev. 20:6.) No one would think the Lord would send Samuel from heaven at the call of a witch. He had ordered the Jews to put them to death, and King Saul had put them to death. The inspired writer has told us what the woman, Saul, and the spirit said, but he does *not* say the

Lord said it was Samuel, and it was not. Then it was the evil spirit who said to Saul, "The Lord will also deliver Israel with thee into the hand of the Philistines; and to-morrow shalt thou and thy sons be with me; the Lord also shall deliver the host of Israel into the hand of the Philistines." (1 Sam. 28:19.) The Lord had allowed the evil spirit to control Saul. And Satan knew the time had come, and he on the morrow could take him home, and then he would be with the spirit that was conversing with him. Saul could not go to heaven with Samuel, and Saul and his sons did not go to the grave as Samuel did. For the Philistines took the body of Saul and the bodies of his sons and burnt them. Saul refused to obey the Lord and had obeyed the evil spirit for twenty-four years. He could not receive any information from the Lord or Samuel, and had gone to a witch to learn his fate; and Saul took a sword, and fell upon it, and took his own life, therefore, he could not go to heaven, but he was to go with the spirit that the witch said was "gods ascending out of the earth." Must we believe it was Samuel because the Bible tells us Samuel said it? Samuel HAD said it before the devil, but that does not prove he said it then. The Bible tells us, "The serpent said unto the woman, Ye shall not surely die." (Gen. 3:4.) It was Satan, not the serpent, said it, and again the ass opened her mouth and spoke to Balaam; it was the angel that spake for the ass, and it was Satan that spoke for Samuel to deceive Saul, and then took the spirit of Saul into the earth with him. **For Saul could not go with Samuel to heaven.**

The woman saw gods, or more than one, ascending out of the earth. They told her she was talking to Saul. And they could have told her to make him believe she had called up Samuel, or an old man covered with a mantle, for this does not agree with what she first said, and she does not call the spirit " gods " after that. She was told to call up Samuel; but she did not call him Samuel when he first came up. And if he did come to Saul, there was no use of his coming in disguise, or of his talking to the witch. He would have talked direct to Saul. Look at the place and the company. The house has a ground floor. It is occupied by the witch and her fat calf. King Saul lay on the earth a coward. Saul's two servants were looking on. Would the prophet Samuel come from heaven to honor that place and company with his presence? We have no account of his coming to the earth since. Dear reader, if you cannot see through the mantle the devil got this witch to throw over him, you could not read the mind of a person well enough to make a living by telling fortunes. From this we learn that King Saul had been forsaken by the Lord, and tried for twenty-four years to kill David. He is then told, by gods called up out of the earth by a witch, the result of the battle on the morrow, and then he and his sons would be in the earth with him. That fulfilled Samuel's prophecy, and which the witch's gods used to make him think it was Samuel.

"Now there was a day when the sons of God came to present themselves before the Lord: and Satan came also among them. And the Lord said unto Satan, Whence comest thou? Then Satan answered the Lord and said, From going to and fro in the earth, and from walking up and down in it." (Job 1: 6, 7.) The Book of Job was written 1,520 years before the birth of Christ. The son of God had children on the earth then, and he was talking with them. And Satan admitted his occupation then was to walk up and down in the earth. And his works will prove he has been, and is, doing the same thing yet. And I think he has made this world his abode long enough to call it his home. And he will be on the earth at the second, and third or last, coming of Christ.

The Lord permitted the devil to afflict Job to show all men he had power to control the devil, and he could not afflict men without the Lord's permission. Men have been, like King Saul, willing to obey the devil. And the Lord has let him afflict them because they did not obey the word of the Lord. Faith and obedience is better than sacrifice.

Satan had control of the Sabeans who slew Job's oxen and asses, and of the fire of God that fell from heaven and burned up the sheep and the servants, and also of the Chaldeans who took the camels, and the wind that smote the house and killed Job's sons, and also of Job's wife when she said to him, "Curse God and die." And he must have controlled Job's friends who were with him seven days and seven nights, and none spake a word unto him. We learn from this that Satan can control men and the elements when the Lord permits him to do it. He did his work in a way to make Job think the Lord was doing it, and Job did think he was when he said, "The Lord gave and the Lord hath taken away." (Job 1 : 21.) But the Lord protected Job and he sinned not. "As for the earth, out of it cometh bread : and under it is turned up as it were fire." (Job 28 : 5.) The grain that grows from the earth we use to make bread. Then in or under the earth is a fire that has never gone out. "The depth saith, Wisdom is not in me, and the sea saith, It is not in me." (Job 28 : 14.) We go down in the deep when we go down in the sea. But in that verse the Lord speaks of another depth, that would go down to the centre of the earth—the end of depths. "He will deliver his soul from going into the pit, and his life shall see the light." (Job 33 : 28.) This does not promise to deliver the body of Christ from going down into the grave. But the Lord would not let his soul go into the bottomless pit. For he was to go up to paradise. "He keepeth back his soul from the pit, and his life from perishing by the sword." (Job 33 : 18.) "He maketh the deep to boil like a pot." (Job 41 : 31.) The sea does not boil, and that must refer to the fire in this earth, for that is called deep.

Christ said to the Jews, "Ye are of your father

the devil." (John 8 : 44.) They are his children for they obey him. Jonah was a prophet, and he refused to obey the Lord's command, and went on board a ship to flee from the work the Lord had told him to do. The Lord followed him. He was thrown into the sea. "And the Lord had prepared a great fish to swallow up Jonah. And Jonah was in the belly of the fish three days and three nights." (Jonah 1 : 17.) "For as Jonas was three days and three nights in the fish's belly, so shall the Son of man be three days and three nights in the heart of the earth." (Matt. 12 : 40.) This refers to the body of Christ, and not his soul, for that went to paradise. And to the body of Jonah and not his soul, for his soul at that time we are told, went into the belly of hell. That chastisement prepared Jonah to do the Lord's work well. And the death and resurrection of Christ prepared him for the great work he came to do for our race.

"Then Jonah prayed unto the Lord his God out of the fish's belly." (Jonah 2 : 1.) "When my soul fainted within me I remembered the Lord; and my prayer came in unto thee, into thine Holy temple." (Jonah 2 : 7.) The words "fainted" and "sleep" are used when the Lord speaks of separating the soul and body. "The waters compassed me about, even to the soul: the depth closed round about, the weeds were wrapped about my head." (Jonah 2 : 5.) "I went down to the bottom of the mountains; the earth with her bars was about me forever: yet hast thou brought up my life from corruption, O Lord, my God." (Jonah 2 : 6.) "And I cried by reason of mine affliction unto the Lord, and he heard me: out of the belly of hell cried I, and thou heardest my voice." (Jonah 2 : 2.) When the weeds were about Jonah's head he must refer to his spiritual body after he had left the fish, and before he went to the bottom of the mountains or down into the belly of hell. And in answer to that prayer the Lord delivered his soul from hell, and his body, like Christ's, did not see corruption; for his soul returned to his body, and, like Christ, he was raised from the dead in three days from the time the fish swallowed him.

It would be a greater miracle for the Lord to keep the soul of Jonah in his body in the fish three days than it would to let the soul go from the body, as the law of nature directs, and then return to it, as the soul of Christ did. If we cannot prove by this that the soul of Jonah left the body and he was raised from the dead, how can we prove that Christ was dead or was raised from the dead. For the law that unites and keeps the soul and body together was as much violated in the one case as it was in the other. And the Lord spake unto the fish, and it vomited out Jonah upon the dry land." (Jonah 2 : 10.) Then the Lord gave Jonah the same command, and he went and obeyed the Lord, and the city of Nineveh was not overthrown.

The Lord told the prophet to say to the King of Babylon, "Hell from beneath is moved for thee to meet thee at thy coming: it stirreth up the dead for thee." (Isa. 14 : 9.) The dead who were to meet the King at his coming must be the souls of those who had gone to the pit before him, and were waiting for and expecting him to come. "All they shall speak and say unto thee, Art thou also become weak as we? Art thou become like unto us? Thy pomp is brought down to the grave, the worm is spread under thee, and the worms cover thee." (Isa. 14 : 10, 11.) His body must have been in the grave then, and his soul gone down into the pit with those who were expecting him. "For thou hast said in thine heart, I will ascend into heaven, I will exalt my throne above the stars of God. I will ascend above the heights of the clouds, I will be like the MOST HIGH. Yet thou shalt be brought down to hell, to the sides of the pit." (Isa. 14 : 13, 14, 15.) The King of Babylon, after he was in the grave with "worms under and over him" could not ascend above the clouds, but must be cast down to hell to the sides of the pit. That must locate the bottomless pit in this earth. This was written by Isaiah one hundred and seventy years before it was fulfilled. "In that night was Belshazzar the King of the Chaldeans slain." (Dan. 5 : 30.) If the prophet could tell the proud kings of Babylon that they would be brought down to the bottomless pit in this earth, and those he had wronged would be glad to see him come to that place of torment deprived of all his wealth and power, the Lord must have revealed it to him. The King should have been instructed by this prophecy, and made wise improvement of the time given him to prepare for the end or the time for its fulfillment. "The Lord shall punish the kings of the earth upon the earth, and they shall be shut up in the prison, and after many days shall they be visited." (Isa. 24 : 21, 22.) The prison in which the kings of the earth are to be shut up for many days must be in this earth, for the kings of the earth are not put in prison in this life, but it is in a future state, and they will be visited and released at the resurrection. But the release or visit will be of short duration. "Praise the Lord from the earth, ye dragons and all deeps." (Psa. 198 : 7.) The bottomless pit is the home of the dragon, and is called all deeps. The pit in this earth is all the prison we have in which the devil could be confined for a thousand years, and where after the end of his release or the last resurrection he will be confined forever. "Whither shall I flee from thy presence? If I ascend up in heaven, thou art there. If I make my bed in hell, behold, thou art there." (Psa. 139 : 7, 8.) Then if we make our bed in hell, we do not ascend up into heaven. If we do not go down in this earth and do not ascend up from it in the air in space called heaven, where do we go to find a place called hell to make our bed in, that could be called a prison or place of confinement filled with everlasting fire like the fire in this earth? "Whatsoever the Lord pleased, that did he in heaven and in the earth, in the seas, and in all deep places." (Psa. 135 : 6.) Why do the prophets say so much about the deep places of the earth if we have no interest in them in time or eternity? David in the 28th Psalm prayed that the Lord would not let him " become like them that go down into the pit." " Let not the water floods overflow me, neither let the deep swallow me up, and let not the pit shut her mouth upon me." (Psa. 59 : 15.) " Blessed be the Lord because he hath heard the voice of my supplication." (Psa. 28 : 6.) David in this life was sure he had the favor and blessing of God. It is not so with the wicked, for " upon the wicked he shall rain snares and brimstone and a horrible tempest; this shall be the portion of their cup." (Psa. 11 : 6.) The pit that David prayed the Lord would deliver him from, and not let him go down into, was not the grave, for he did go to the grave; neither was it the trials he was called to pass through in this life. But the Holy Spirit taught him to pray to be delivered from going down into the bottomless pit or to the devil's abode, when he went into a future state. And the prayers of David are recorded in God's Word to instruct and encourage all men. " He that believeth not God hath made him a liar." (1 John 5 : 10.) " Let God be true, if that makes every man a liar." (Romans 3 : 4.) " And all liars shall have their part in the lake which burneth with fire and brimstone, which is the second death." (Rev. 21 : 8.) That will be an eternal separation from all who are in heaven, and from all who live or stay on the earth after the last coming of Christ; then his offer of salvation ends. "How shall we escape if we neglect so great salvation?" (Heb. 2:3.) "That through death he might destroy him that had the power of death, that is, the devil, and deliver them." (Heb. 2:14.) Christ came from heaven to this, the devil's home, to free men from his control. When we see how unwilling the god of this world is to lose control of his subjects, and how unwilling men are to secure this great salvation, we can form some idea of the value he places on the service of men, and the value the Son of God has placed on their deliverance. He has told all men he will save them if they will OBEY and SERVE him. And those who will not serve him as they are instructed in his word to serve him in this life will be confined in this earth, and the curse will be on them as they dwell in that pit or prison. "And the smoke of their torment ascendeth up for ever and ever." (Rev. 14:11.) And as the smoke from all the sacrifices that had been offered to the God of heaven from Adam to Christ ascended up in space called heaven, so the smoke from the prison or pit in this earth could ascend up forever in the heaven that will be around the earth then. Christ came down from heaven to the earth, and went up from the earth when he went back to heaven. He does not tell us in his Word that the lost will be taken from this earth, but he tells us in plain words that they must go down into a bottomless pit.

"And he dreamed, and behold a ladder set up on the earth, and the top of it reached to heaven, and, behold, the angels of God ascending and descending on it; and, behold, the Lord stood above it, and said, I am the Lord God of Abraham, thy father, and the God of Isaac." (Gen. 28 : 12, 13.) That ladder is Christ. The devil, his angels, and the lost will not go up to heaven on the promises or on the work of Christ; for they will not obey him, or be governed by his word in this life, and will not consent for him to dwell in and rule over them, for they are under the control of their father, the devil, and he deceives them, and they know it not. If the devil has a ladder on which he and his can leave this earth and go to some other part of space, it has not been revealed to us in the Word of God. If men will believe what the Lord has told them in his Word about the location of the devil's home, and the description he has given of it, they will never think of leaving this earth and going up in space to find it. If men believe what the Lord has told them about other things, why not believe what he has written in his Word on this subject? The Lord is the author of all language, and he must understand the meaning of the words he has ordered used in pointing to and in describing the bottomless pit, prepared for the home of the devil and all the lost. "Woe unto them that call evil good, and good evil; that put darkness for light, and light for darkness." That woe must rest on every person who refuses to believe any truth plainly taught in the

Bible. It is not *enough* for us to believe what men tell us is good, or good *enough* to prepare us for heaven, if it is not what *the Lord* has told us to do in his Word. For the Lord has said, many will strive to enter in, and will not be able. The Lord has promised eternal life to all who believe his Word and obey his commands. The promise is not to those who obey the commands of men and believe what men tell them they must do to inherit eternal life. For men often put darkness for light. We can know the spirit that controls us by the instruction it gives; any spirit that tells us not to believe all we find in the Word of God we should say is not the right spirit.

The Creator of heaven and earth tells men in his Word they must look up to heaven, climb up to heaven, go up above the clouds to heaven, and calls all space above and around the earth heaven, up to the third heaven; and then tells men who live on the earth they must go down into hell, down in the nether parts of the earth, in a prison he has prepared for the devil and his angels, who have made this earth their abode. And we have no words that will describe the interior of this earth better than the words used to describe hell. The reason men give for not believing this is that they do not know where hell is, and do not want to know, for they do not intend to go to that place. I think that is a very poor excuse for not believing what the Lord has told us in his Word about it: "For he hath looked down from the height of his sanctuary, from heaven did the Lord behold the earth." (Psa. 102 : 19.) Heaven and height is the opposite to down. "Of old hast thou laid the foundation of the earth, and the heavens are the work of thy hands." (Psa. 102 : 25.) This tells us the Lord created more than one heaven, and it is as important to create the third heaven around this system of worlds as it was to create the air around the earth and call it heaven. "For as the heaven is high above the earth, so great is his mercy toward them that fear him." (Psa. 103 : 11.) This must point to the third heaven, for it speaks of a heaven far above the earth. "The Lord is high above all nations, and his glory above the heavens and the earth." (Psa. 113 : 4.) If the Lord is above the heavens and the earth, is he not above the devil and his home? "Faith, if it hath not works, is dead being alone." (Jas. 2 : 17.) We may believe there is one God and one heaven, if that faith does not give us wisdom to understand and believe what is revealed to us in God's Word, and make us willing to obey his commands: will that faith prepare us for heaven, if it does not prepare us to do what the Lord calls good works while we are on this earth?

"Ye shall know them by their fruit." (Matt. 7 : 16.) The fruit of the Holy Spirit is not intended to make us believe what men tell us, if it is not revealed to us in the Word of God. "For broad is the way that leadeth to destruction, and many there be which go in thereat." (Matt. 7 : 13.) How few men there are living on the earth who believe this, and include themselves in the number who are going down the road to destruction. "The spirit of the beast that goeth downward." (Eccles. 3 : 21.) "He that committeth sin is of the devil, for the devil sinneth from the beginning." (1 John 3 : 8.) If we do not believe this, and all the Lord has told us about the devil's home, is not the devil the author of that unbelief? We can gain nothing by permitting him to blind, deceive, and control us. We should remember that the fear of the Lord is the beginning of wisdom, and it is our duty and to our interest to believe all the Lord has revealed to us in his Word, for it is given to us for our good; and the Lord could make no mistake when he tells us we must go down to find hell, for he created it, and drove the devil down from heaven to the earth, and then told us we must go down from the outside of the earth we are on, to find the prison in which they are to be confined forever.

Some may think the quotations I have selected to prove the points in this book could be changed by what is written before and after them; they cannot if we compare them to what was said about Christ's first coming or any fulfilled prophecy. This world must be everlasting if the soul lives forever, and the home prepared for the lost is everlasting. For the Holy Spirit has ordered the same words used when he tells us all God's works are everlasting. Some of his works may be changed by fire, and some by decomposition, but it remains in another form, and is not destroyed, and will be everlasting. He has created the human body from the dust of the earth, and to dust it shall return. The Lord has created our earthly body, and it is a temporal home for the soul, which he tells us will exist forever, and it must be the intelligent part of our being. It can be changed from good to evil, and the Lord can change it from evil to good; and the Lord will change this sin-smitten world from its present condition to a sinless paradise for spiritual beings that will not be changed forever.

The world will be changed, but it must remain a world forever in a re-created state. "For all the land which thou seest, to thee will I give it, and to thy seed forever." (Gen. 13 : 15.)

The descendants of Abraham have not occupied that land for many years; but the time will come when they will occupy it forever in a recreated state. "The Lord did swear by himself that he would multiply the seed of Abraham as the stars of heaven, and all this land that I have spoken of will I give unto your seed, and they shall inherit it forever." (Ex. 32 : 13.) Abraham and many of his descendants are in paradise on a visit, and they will return to that land when the Lord recreates it, and he will recreate them, and make it their everlasting home. "That thou mayest prolong thy days upon the earth, which the Lord thy God giveth thee, forever." (Deut. 4 : 40.) In this verse the Lord tells them how they can prolong their temporal stay on the earth, and then tells them he will in time give it to them forever. "And Moses sware on that day, saying, Surely the land whereon thy feet have trodden shall be thine inheritance and thy children's forever." (Josh. 14 : 9.) This promise, in God's time, must be fulfilled; and if we are God's children, we will see it fulfilled, "and dwell in the land that the Lord hath given unto you and to your fathers for ever and ever." (Jer. 25 : 5.) "Then will I cause you to dwell in this place, in the land that I gave to your fathers for ever and ever." (Jer. 7 : 7.) "And the seventh angel sounded; and there were great voices in heaven, saying, The kingdoms of this world are become the kingdoms of our Lord and of his Christ; and he shall reign for ever and ever." (Rev. 11 : 15.) "And there shall be no night there, and they need no candles, neither light of the sun: for the Lord God giveth them light; and they shall reign for ever and ever." (Rev. 22 : 5.) "He stood and measured the earth; he beheld, and drove asunder the nations; and the everlasting mountains were scattered, the perpetual hills did bow; his ways are everlasting." (Hab. 3 : 6.) "The hills melted like wax at the presence of the Lord of the whole earth." (Psa. 97 : 5.) This will be done at the third coming of Christ, to put death under his feet, stop the multiplication of Adam's race on the earth, and make all things new; and all who are saved are like the angels in heaven, then, and the recreated earth will be everlasting.

There is nothing on the earth that annihilates created matter. Fire causes the rapid decomposition of chemicals, but it does not destroy matter. It changes what has been drawn together by the laws of nature, but the created matter of which it has been composed remains in some other form. We purify many things we find in the earth with fire. It is not consumed; for the gold and the dross remain. We melt sand, and it is changed to glass; the earth may be melted like wax and changed to glass; *that does not* consume created matter, or remove the foundations of the earth. For the Lord has told us they will not be removed forever. All the earth produces by the laws of nature is not a new creation; it is changing what had been created into other forms; all this must decompose or be changed. The grain we sow decomposes and produces other grain; our body returns to dust, but it will be raised a spiritual body that will endure forever. We have nothing in the Bible or in the laws of nature that would give us any reason to suppose that the created matter of this earth and the air that is all around it will ever pass away. And the redeemed will live on the earth, and the lost will be sealed up in it, and the lake of fire that is now and will then be in it will be everlasting. If we wish to live on it, then we must fear the Lord in this life, believe what he has told us in his Word, and keep his commandments. For all that is said about the world by the Creator of all things must and will be fulfilled.

Jacob, in his blessing to Joseph, calls the hills " everlasting hills." (Gen. 49 : 26.)

I think this proves to us the earth that now surrounds the lake of fire that is in it will be everlasting walls around it. The fire in the earth could be called a lake of fire surrounded by land. "And death and hell were cast into the lake of fire. This is the second death." (Rev. 20 : 14.) I find nothing in the Bible that would give me any reason to suppose I had any right to look for another prison or lake of fire in which the devil and the lost could be confined forever. And all the Bible tells us about the home of the lost would be fulfilled if we take the lake of fire in this earth and call it the prison in which they are to be confined. And I think it is our duty to believe it, or give some reason for not believing it, TAKEN FROM THE BIBLE.

What object can the Lord have, or what other reason has he given, for keeping the fire burning for so many thousands of years if he has no use for it? It is of no use to anything that lives on the earth. And the Lord has told us that he has prepared a place of that kind, and the road that leads to it he has told us " is a broad road, and many there be that go in thereat." For the god of this world has blinded the minds of men in all ages of the world, so they could not see or understand what the Lord had revealed to them in his Word for their good. Some account for the fire in the earth by believing a theory that this earth came from the sun in a melted state, and that the outside has cooled and become hard, and the interior of the earth is in a melted state yet. That theory conflicts with all the Creator has told us about his creating the air, the water, and laying of the foundation of the earth, and that it was not to be removed forever. And all we know of the crust of the earth proves to us that it was created in or under water, as there is water in all that is created. And if the earth had been melted our rocks would not have had so much water in them. And the different kinds of rocks we have on the earth would have been mixed up, and our soil that is worn from the rocks when they were new and in a soft state would all be alike; and the water would not remain on the surface of the earth, or so near it that it is within the reach of man, and all that live on the earth. And the law of attraction would not permit the world to leave the sun, for that law keeps the water on the earth, and when water is drawn up in the air by the sun, it returns again to the earth, drawn by that law. And the size of the sun gives it a power to attract many thousands of times greater than the earth's attraction, and if one world, or all the planets in this system, did come from the sun, the law of attraction would be gone, and the sun would form a million worlds and scatter off in space. I do not see how any one can give a reason for believing that theory.

I would give all who believe the earth came from the sun the advice a father gave his little girl when she asked him if the moon was made of green cheese. He told her to go and see what the Bible said about the creation of the moon. She read what the Lord has told us about the creation of all in this system of worlds, and returned to her father and told him the Lord created the moon before he created the cows; therefore the moon could not be made of cheese.

The Lord tells us he created the earth before he created the sun and moon ; therefore, the world could not come from the sun if it was created first. In the beginning God created the air and the earth. That may refer to his beginning to create this earth, and the earth may be the first thing created in this system of worlds. It would require no more divine power to create the earth than it would to turn "Lot's wife into a pillar of salt" (Gen. 19 : 26), or protect "three men in a furnace of fire exceeding hot." (Dan. 3 : 22.) And it would take as much power to control the nations of the earth, and make them fulfill, or do, all he has told the prophets to say that they would do, or to know that Peter would deny him thrice, and then know his faith would fail not. "Mine hand also hath laid the foundation of the earth, and my right hand hath spanned the heavens." (Isa. 48 : 13.) "Of old thou hast laid the foundation of the earth." (Psalms 102 : 25.) "Who laid the foundations of the earth, that it should not be removed forever." (Prov. 104 : 5.) This makes the foundations of the world everlasting, and nothing said about the earth coming from the sun.

The evil spirit persuaded men to reject the preaching of Christ and his apostles ; and also Martin Luther and his co-workers in the Reformation. And he persuaded men who claimed to be God's children to persecute John Bunyan and thousands of other good men, who were led by the spirit of God to do what they did. It is the evil spirit that will not in this day let men understand the Bible as it is revealed by its author. He has divided the so-called Christian Church up into many branches ; and he makes some men believe some of Christ's commands are not essential to salvation, and they need not obey them. Men should not be governed by any spirit that conflicts with or misconstrues the Word of God. If there is nothing in the Bible that conflicts with what is presented in this book, and if it accords with its teachings, what reason can be given for refusing to believe it, and would any excuse free men when they are called before the Judge of all the earth ? For he has given us the Bible, and he has told us the devil is opposed to it and does not want us to understand or believe it. And we are told in his Word to watch and pray, for the devil has, and is, deceiving many of our race. And the lost would warn the living, if they could, not to come to that place of torment. And those in heaven would invite all to come and join that happy throng forever. Reader, do it ; for if you refuse or neglect to obey the commands of the Lord, who has created and controls all things, you must spend a never-ending eternity in the fire which is, and will be, in this earth forever. For the Lord has revealed it, and he changes not, and his word must all be fulfilled. The evil spirit may make you believe this is all a humbug, but that will not change the word of God as to the home of the lost. This is not intended to frighten men, but it is to show them what salvation is worth to them, and what it is to be lost forever. Men can gain nothing in this life by serving "the god of this world," but eternal torment forever in a future state.

The Son of God is as willing to save men now as he was when he was on the earth. And he can say now, as he did then, "Ye would not." At his last coming this will change : men will be willing then, but he will not. It will pay all men to search the Word of God and give it a literal interpretation. Believe what is revealed ; obey the commands ; " hunger and thirst after righteousness ;" prove to all men you have Christ's spirit by your works. Turn from "the god of this world" and serve him not. Then, at the end of life's journey, you can leave this sinful world and ascend to the third heaven, and return with Christ at his last coming, to renovate the earth, free it from sin, and confine the devil and all his works in the earth forever. Reader, where will you be then ?

THE FIRST COMING OF CHRIST TO MAKE A SACRIFICE FOR SIN.

THE period from Christ's First Coming to his Second is and will be fulfilled prophecy. I will call his birth in Bethlehem his first coming. For then he came in our nature, and was called the "second Adam, the Lord from heaven."

He was born under the law, and was without sin, so he could save his people from their sins. And we are told he will be "the first-born among many brethren." That coming was an important event in the world's history; for as Abraham looked for the promised son, so all the generations of men from Adam had looked for the Messiah to come "to bruise the serpent's head," and permit Satan "to bruise his heel." And Abraham told his son Isaac when he was preparing to offer him to the Lord for a sacrifice that "God would provide a lamb for an offering," and that lamb was a substitute for Christ, who would come from him, or from his seed. "For in thy seed shall all the nations of the earth be blessed." (Gen. 22 : 18.) And all the sacrifices that had been offered to the Lord by men (if they offered them as the Lord commanded them to do) pointed to that coming of Christ, and this coming, and the sacrifice he made, was to be the end of that law. And it ended with the overthrow of Jerusalem, and the scattering of the Jews among all nations.

Satan must have told Cain to offer "the fruit of the ground for an offering unto the Lord." (Gen. 4 : 3.) For Paul has told us, "without shedding of blood is no remission." (Heb. 9 : 22.) And the history of Cain proves he had obeyed Satan, and in that way had become his servant, and was controlled by him, and therefore slew his brother. This should be a warning to all who think they have a right to change or refuse to believe the Word of God. Jesus at his first coming did all the prophets had said he would do at that time. And if they had not told of his second coming, and what he would do then, the Jews would have believed on him. For they were looking for the Messiah to come, and fulfill that part of prophecy that will be fulfilled at his second coming — at which time he will come and do all the prophets said he would do for the Jews. Jesus said, "This gospel of the kingdom shall be preached in all the world for a witness unto all nations, and then shall the end come." (Matt. 24 : 14.) I think a part of this prophecy is fulfilled. The gospel is to be preached to the end of the world, to all nations; but Jesus had told his disciples of another end that does not refer to the end of the world. All the evangelists, in this connection, tell us that Jesus had been telling the Jews that the temple would be thrown down and not one stone left on another. "And they asked him, When shall these things be?" And one answer he gave them is this: "And when ye shall see Jerusalem compassed with armies, then know that the desolation thereof is nigh." (Luke 21 : 20.) "For these be the days of vengeance, that all things which are written may be fulfilled." And the scattering of the Jews had been plainly written: "And they shall fall by the edge of the sword; and shall be led away captive into all nations; and Jerusalem shall be trodden down of the Gentiles, until the times of the Gentiles be fulfilled." (Luke 21 : 22, 24.) Then Jesus goes on and tells them about His last coming, and what will be done then. He tells them the time of the Gentiles will end, and that before the end of the world, or end of the age, all that the prophets have told about the history of the Jews, and of Jerusalem and its overthrow, and the scattering of the Jews among all nations, has been fulfilled at his first coming, or will be before his second coming. Jesus knew the Jews would put him to death to save the Jewish nation and their religion. But he told them his gospel, that they would not believe or receive, would be preached in all the world, or to all the nations (and *it will be* to the end of time). But then Jesus told them that the end of the temple, Jerusalem, and the Jewish nation they wanted to preserve, would come, and when it came his gospel had been preached to all the nations known to them, and in which they would be scattered. And that was the end of the Jewish dispensation, and the gospel of Christ had taken its place. And the Jews have had no king or flag around which they could rally, or a country they could call their own, from that time to this, and they will not till Christ's second coming. If we wish to understand prophecy we must understand the history of the world as it is revealed to us by the prophets, and if we review the past it will help us to understand the future. There have been changes in the past, and there will be in the future.

The first period in the world's history I will call from the creation of man to the Flood. The second period of time was from the Flood to the birth of Jesus. And the third from his birth to his second coming. Nearly all prophecy which was to be fulfilled in this dispensation has been fulfilled. And the fourth or next change will be the thousand years the devil is to be confined, and not permitted to deceive men. And the fifth period of time will be from the devil's release to the third coming of Christ, to raise the dead and make all things new. During that time the devil is loosed from his prison, and he will deceive men who live on the earth. Then Christ will come and confine the devil and all his works in everlasting fires forever. That will be the end of prophecy, and the end of the multiplication of Adam's race; for then the redeemed will be like the angels in heaven, not married nor given in marriage. Then Jesus can conquer death, and put all enemies under his feet forever. By this we can see what prophecy was to be fulfilled in the time of the Jewish sacrifice; and what prophecy will be fulfilled in this age of the world; and what will be while the devil is confined. And we have some prophecy left to be fulfilled after the devil is loosed for a season. And all prophecy is to be fulfilled before Satan is confined forever, so that he cannot harm the redeemed who will live on a re-created earth surrounded by a new heaven.

The prophets had told the Jews what would be done by Christ at his first coming. But they were more interested in what they had told them about his second coming, and they overlooked all they had told them about his first coming, as a lamb that had been promised would be slain for the remission of sin from the fall of man.

When Jacob blessed his sons he said, "The sceptre shall not depart from Judah, nor a lawgiver from between his feet; until Shiloh come; and unto him shall the gathering of the people be." (Gen. 49 : 10.) This refers to Christ's first coming. He came then to scatter the Jews among all nations, and he must come again to gather them on earth. He does not mean the redeemed in heaven. He has not done that yet. When Christ was born Judah had no king, and the sceptre had departed from them, and they had no lawgiver, and they were looking for the Messiah to come. And the angel of the Lord told Joseph to " call his name Jesus, for he shall save his people from their sins." His birth troubled Herod and all Jerusalem, for they supposed he was born for a king. And the angel of the Lord told Joseph to take the young child into Egypt, for Herod would seek to destroy him. And Herod sent and slew all the children in Bethlehem, as the prophet Jeremiah had said he would. And when Herod was dead an angel of the Lord told Joseph to take the child and his mother into the land of Israel. And he came and dwelt in Nazareth, as the prophets had said he would. And the angel of the Lord told the shepherds to " Fear not, for unto you is born this day, in the city of David, a Saviour, which is Christ the Lord." (Luke 2 : 11.) And he will be a king at his next coming. And the Holy Ghost had told good old Simeon that he should not see death before he had seen the Lord's Christ; "and he came by the spirit into the temple, and took him up in his arms, and blessed God and said, Lord, now lettest thou thy servant depart in peace, according to thy word, for mine eyes have seen thy salvation." (Luke 2 : 26–30.) " And there was with the angels a multitude of the heavenly host praising God, saying, Glory to God in the highest, and on earth peace, good-will to men." (Luke 2 : 13, 14.) " Christ came not to send peace, but a sword " then. (Matt. 10 : 34.) He will bring peace at his next coming to all men. His birth was in a stable ; but angels were sent from heaven to introduce him to a fallen world. If we read his history from his birth to the cross, as we find it recorded by inspired men who were eye-witnesses to those wonderful works, and then remember that he must have done a hundred good things where one is recorded, we can say with the centurion, "Truly, this man was the Son of God" (Mark 15 : 39), and the second Adam from heaven. He had told his apostles about his death. Judas was to betray him; he was to be raised from the grave the third day. He appeared to the apostles, and when he was parted from them and ascended up in heaven the angel told them he would return in like manner. He proved his divinity, and proved, by his works and what he said, he was a prophet. And the Father called him his son and told us to hear him. The prophet "said unto them, If ye think good, give me my price, and if not, forbear, so they weighed for my son's price thirty pieces of silver. And the Lord said unto me, Cast unto the potter a goodly price that I was prized at of them." (Zech. 11 : 12, 13.) "Then Judas, who had betrayed him, seeing that he was condemned, repented and returned the thirty pieces of silver to the chief priests and elders, saying, I have sinned in betraying innocent blood. And they said, What is that to us? see thou to that. And he threw down the pieces of silver in the temple and departed; and he went and hanged himself." (Matt. 27 : 3, 4, 5.) *All* that the prophets had said would be done to the Son of God when he came on the earth was as literally fulfilled as that was. Again as to this: "And the chief priests, taking the silver pieces, said,

It is not lawful to put them into the treasury, since they are the price of blood. And having taken counsel, they bought with them the potter's field, as a burial-place for strangers. Wherefore that field was called the field of blood. And they gave them for the potter's field." (Matt. 27 : 6, 7, 8, 9, 10.) And again, Christ had said to the prophets, by the Holy Spirit : " I gave my back to the smiters, and my cheeks to them that plucked off the hair; I hid not my face from shame and spitting." (Isa. 50 : 6.) "Then did they spit in his face, and buffeted him; and others smote him with the palms of their hands." (Matt. 26 : 67.) " He keepeth all his bones, not one of them is broken." (Psa. 34 : 20.) "They brake not his legs." (John 19 : 33.) "They pierced my hands and my feet. I may tell all my bones, they look and stare upon me." (Psa. 22 : 16, 17.) "They part my garments among them and cast lots upon my vesture." (Psa. 22 : 18.) "The soldiers took his garments and made four parts, to every soldier a part; the coat was without seam, woven throughout, and they cast lots for it." (John 19 : 23.) "They gave me also gall for my meat, and in my thirst they gave me vinegar to drink." (Psa. 69 : 21.) " The chief priests mocking him, with the scribes and elders, said, If he be the king of Israel, let him now come down from the cross and we will believe him." (Matt. 27 : 42.) Christ came from the grave, but the priests did not believe on him, and they were not willing that the people should. "For they gave large money unto the soldiers, saying, Say ye, His disciples came by night and stole him away while we slept. And if this come to the governor's ears, we will persuade him and secure you." (Matt. 28 : 13, 14.)

It will be seen by this, and many other references that could be made, how literally all this was fulfilled in the crucifixion of Christ. This proves the Lord can control the devil, and all men who serve him, and who are controlled by him. We learn from this and all the Jews did to Christ, the power which Satan has over men when the Lord permits him to use it to control them. "And they said, Let his blood be on us and our children." And that prayer was answered, and more than six hundred years before the overthrow of Jerusalem the Lord told the prophets to tell them about it. The Lord told Ezekiel to take the hair from his head and divide it in three parts. He was to burn a third part in the city in the days of the siege, and a third part he was to smite with a knife; and a third part thou shalt scatter in the wind; and I will draw out a sword after them. "Thou shalt also take a few in number and bind them in thy skirts, and cast them in the fire and burn them. Thus saith the Lord God: This is Jerusalem. Behold, I, even I, am against thee, and I will execute judgment in the midst of thee, in the sight of the nations. Therefore the fathers shall eat their sons in the midst of thee, and the sons shall eat their fathers; and I will execute judgment in thee, and the whole remnant of thee will I scatter into all the winds. I will not spare, neither will I have any pity. A third part of thee shall die with the pestilence, and with famine; and a third part shall fall by the sword, and I will scatter a third part into all the winds. I will make thee waste and a reproach among the nations that are round about thee." This is from the 5th chapter of Ezekiel. "And I will sow them among the people, and they shall remember me in far countries; and they shall live with their children." (Zech. 10: 9.) All this is before Christ's second coming. "And the remnant of Jacob shall be in the midst of many people, as a dew from the Lord. And the remnant of Jacob shall be among the Gentiles in the midst of many people." (Micah. 5 : 7, 8.) They are in all parts of the world now. "For I will gather all nations against Jerusalem to battle, and the city shall be taken, and the houses rifled, and the women ravished." (Zech. 14 : 2.) "For, lo, I will command, and I will sift the house of Israel among all nations like as corn is sifted in a sieve." (Amos 8: 9.) The Lord did this. "For the children of Israel shall abide many days without a king, and without a prince, and without a sacrifice, and without an image, and without ephod. and without teraphim." They are without all this yet. "Afterward shall the children of Israel return and seek the Lord their God, and David their king; and shall fear the Lord and his goodness in the latter days." (Hos. 3 : 4, 5.) They will do this at Christ's second coming.

THE FIRST COMING OF CHRIST. 91

The Jews were scattered among all nations about seventy years after the birth of Christ. They had never been scattered in all nations before. They are scattered now, and have been from that time to this, and will be till the second coming of Christ. They will be without a king or a sacrifice until he comes to them, and then they will return to him with weeping and with supplication. They must return to him on this earth, and it must be before the earth is made new at the third coming of Christ, and the general judgment, and the last resurrection; it will be too late to return to Christ then; no time to do then what the prophets have told us they will do in Jerusalem. Christ will have no time then to do for the Jews, and for all the nations of the earth, what he has promised to do for them on the earth before the end comes. I do not understand how men can read in the Bible all the Lord has promised to do for the Jews, as a nation, and see how faithful he has been to fulfill his promises in the past, and then read what the same prophets have told us the Lord would do for them in the future on this earth, and on the land he gave to their fathers, and believe it will or can be fulfilled in a future state and not on this earth.

Christ, at his first coming, is called a lamb, and what he did at that coming proves it to be an appropriate name for him. At his second coming he is called a king and the "Prince of Peace" (Isa. 9: 6), and that represents what he will do then. At his third coming he will be a king and the "Lion of the tribe of Judah," with all things put under him. That includes the devil, sin, and death, with all who refuse to be governed by his revealed law, and have not had his spirit to guide them in the way of truth. "If any man have not the spirit of Christ, he is none of his" (Rom. 8 : 9); and it is his spirit that will enable us to understand his Word.

CHRIST'S SECOND COMING.

"TO BE A KING AND THE PRINCE OF PEACE."

CHRIST'S second coming will be the next important event in the world's history. We are not to know the day or year he will come, but we have unfulfilled prophecy that could not be fulfilled in this dispensation, and could not be in a future state; and Christ has told us he will come when the fullness of the Gentiles comes in and do all he has promised to do for the Jewish nation. "And when Jesus was taken up into heaven two men in white apparel said, Ye men of Galilee, why stand ye gazing up into heaven? This same Jesus which is taken up from you into heaven shall so come in like manner as ye have seen him go into heaven." (Acts 1:11.) When Jesus was parted from his disciples and taken up into heaven, he was in a human body so he could converse with men, and the angel was sent to tell them he would return in like manner. He was called Lord in the Old Testament, and the inspired writers tell us he visited the earth in what appeared to be a human body, from Adam to the days of Abraham.

At the request of Abraham he promised to spare Sodom if he could find ten righteous men in the city, but they could not be found. Abraham and his wife appeared to know the Lord at that time, and were not surprised at anything he said to them. If a stranger had come and said what the Lord did about the promised son and the overthrow of Sodom, they would have both been surprised, and wanted to know who he was, and who sent him to say and do those things. Christ will not come to condemn men at his second coming, for all who live on the earth then will rejoice, and all the redeemed in heaven with the angelic host will shout for joy, for they know that the devil is to be confined for a thousand years, and that must add to the joys of heaven and earth, for all will know the Lord then, from the least to the greatest, who live on the earth. John, in a vision, saw what would be done on the earth before the end of the world, as it is, and it will all be done. "And John saw an angel come down from heaven, having the key of the bottomless pit and a great chain in his hand. And he laid hold on the dragon, that old serpent which is the devil and Satan, and bound him a thousand years, and cast him into the bottomless pit and shut him up, and set a seal upon him that he should deceive the nations no more till the thousand years should be fulfilled. And after that he must be loosed a little season." That season may be as long as the time from Christ's first to his second coming, for Jesus called that time short. And the souls John saw were those who had been beheaded for the witness of Jesus, and will have part in the first resurrection; and they will reign with Christ on the earth a thousand years. "But the rest of the dead lived not again until the thousand years were finished." (Rev. 20 : 1–5.) His twelve apostles may have part in the first resurrection, for Jesus said to them, "When the Son of man shall sit in the throne of his glory, ye shall sit upon twelve thrones, judging the twelve tribes of Israel." (Matt. 19 : 28.) They have been in heaven over eighteen hundred years, and the reign of a thousand years must refer to some other time. They may come with Christ and judge the twelve tribes of Israel, who live on the earth, for a thousand years after Christ's second coming. "And I appoint unto you a kingdom, as my father has appointed unto me, that ye may eat and drink at my table in my kingdom, and sit on thrones judging the twelve tribes of Israel." (Luke 22 : 29, 30.) That may be on this earth. I would not suppose the redeemed in heaven would want judging in tribes, and eat and drink at a table called Christ's table. "Christ was once offered to bear the sins of many; and unto them that look for him shall he appear the SECOND time without sin unto salvation." (Heb. 9 : 28.) In this Paul teaches us that Christ will come the second time. He has not come yet; and at his third and last coming he will not give salvation to men. He comes then to judge them for what has been done. "I will laugh at your calamity, I will mock when your fear cometh." (Prov. 1 : 26.) Christ will give salvation to all who live on the earth when he confines the devil at his second coming. This could not refer to his third coming, for then all who have salvation will be saved, and all who have not will be lost. And if it refers to their judging the twelve tribes of Israel on a re-created earth, they would judge them then forever. But we are taught by all the prophets that all these things will be fulfilled in the history of the world before the end of our race comes.

"And it shall come to pass when ye be multiplied and increased in the land, in those days, saith the Lord, they shall say no more, The ark of the covenant of the Lord; neither shall it come to mind, neither shall they remember it, neither shall they visit it, neither shall that be done any more." This will be done on the earth before the end comes. "At that time they shall call Jerusalem the throne of the Lord; and all nations shall be gathered unto it, to the name of the Lord, to Jerusalem; neither shall they walk any more after the imagination of their evil heart. In those days the house of Judah shall walk with the house of Israel, and they shall come together out of the land of the north, to the land that I have given for an inheritance unto your fathers." (Jer. 3: 16, 17, 18.) This has not been fulfilled. They do not come from heaven, or go to heaven, but they come from the land in which they are scattered, to the land the Lord had given to their fathers, and he has promised to give it to their children. "For I will take you from among the heathen and gather you out of all countries, and will bring you into your own land." This could not be done at Christ's last coming.

"A new heart also will I give you, and a new spirit will I put within you; and I will take away the stony heart out of your flesh, and I will give you a heart of flesh." The Lord will not give them a heart of flesh in heaven, or after the resurrection. "And I will put my spirit within you, and cause you to walk in my statutes, and ye shall keep my judgments and do them. And ye shall dwell in the land that I gave to your fathers; and ye shall be my people, and I will be your God." (Ezek. 36 : 26, 27, 28.) "And in the days of these kings shall the God of heaven set up a kingdom, which shall never be destroyed; and the kingdom shall not be left to other people, but it shall break in pieces and consume all these kingdoms, and it shall stand forever." Christ is the stone cut out of the mountain without hands. He is a king, and will have a kingdom on this earth for ever. (Dan. 2 : 44.)

Christ's kingdom was set up in the hearts of men at his first coming. And it will be set up in Jerusalem, and in the hearts of all who live on the earth, at his second coming. And when the devil is released he will not break down that kingdom. And at the end of the world it will be established forever in the new Jerusalem, that will come down from heaven, on a re-created earth purified by fire, and surrounded by a new heaven. "And I saw a new heaven and a new earth: for the first heaven and the first earth were passed away, and there was no more sea." (Rev. 21 : 1.) "And I saw, as it were, a sea of glass mingled with fire, and them that had gotten the victory over the beast stand on the sea of glass, having the harps of God. And they sing the song of Moses, the servant of God, and the song of the Lamb." (Rev. 15 : 2, 3.)

This will be done after the third coming of Christ, and I quote it here to show that the prophecy to be fulfilled at the second coming of Christ could not be fulfilled when the world is in that state, and the devil will not be loosed to deceive the nations of the earth after that time. I mean after the third coming of Christ. And at Christ's second coming "he will return unto Zion, and will dwell in the midst of Jerusalem; and Jerusalem shall be called, A city of truth; and the mountain of the Lord of hosts, The holy mountain. Thus saith the Lord of hosts: There shall yet old men and old women dwell in the streets of Jerusalem, and every man with his staff in his hand for very age. And the streets of the city shall be full of boys and girls playing in the streets thereof" (Zech. 8: 3, 4, 5), and must refer to Christ's second coming, for he will return unto Zion and dwell in Jerusalem. He calls the mountains his, and calls them holy. It could not be the new world, for he has told us the old and the young will be in the streets of Jerusalem. That has not been fulfilled yet. "Thus saith the Lord of hosts: If it be marvellous in the eyes of the remnant of this people in these days, should it also be marvellous in mine eyes? saith the Lord of hosts. The Lord will save his people from the east country, and from the west country, and I will bring them, and they shall dwell in the midst of Jerusalem ; and they shall be my people, and I will be their God in truth and in righteousness." (Zech. 8 : 6, 7, 8.)

This has not been done. But the Lord has told us he will do it; and he will bring them from the east and west country, that is, not from heaven. And he does not take them to heaven, for he takes them to Jerusalem, and he will be their God. "And I will bring the third part through the fire, and I will refine them as silver is refined, and will try them as gold is tried; they shall call on my name, and I will hear them; I will say, It is my people: and they shall say, The Lord is my God." (Zech. 13 : 9.) They have not done that yet. "The Lord's house shall be established in the top of the mountain, and all nations shall flow unto it. And many people shall say, Let us go up to the house of the God of Jacob, and he will teach us of his ways, and we will walk in his paths, for out of Zion shall go forth the law and the word of the Lord from Jerusalem. And he shall judge among the nations, and shall rebuke many people, and they shall beat their swords into ploughshares, and their spears into pruning-hooks; nation shall not lift up sword against nation, neither shall they learn war any more." (Isa. 2 : 3, 4.) The Lord speaks to men on the earth. They have swords and spears; they go up to Jerusalem to learn the ways of the Lord; they want plows, and will not learn war any more in the thousand years the devil is confined. And the Lord will judge among other nations, and rebuke many people. This could not be done in heaven. And this state of things on the earth will have an end, for at the end of the world men will be very wicked. After Satan is loosed out of his prison, and before the end of the world comes, "Satan will gather together to battle a large army, the number of whom is as the sand of the sea. And they went up on the breadth of the earth, and compassed the camp of the saints about, and the beloved city; and fire came down from God out of heaven, and devoured them." And at the end of the world, the devil who deceived them, or persuaded them to go and make war on Jerusalem, will be "cast into the lake of fire and brimstone, and he shall be tormented for ever and ever." (Rev. 20 : 8, 9, 10.)

This is the devil's second confinement. The first was for a thousand years. It is evident it will take thousands of years to fulfill the prophecy in those few verses. The prophets record events that will take place, and do not tell us how long a time it will be between the events. We can see what the devil has persuaded men to do; and when he is confined men do not learn war; and when he is loosed from his prison, men engage in war again. Zechariah tells us another army will go to make war on Jerusalem after the release of the devil. For it has not been done, and could not now, for there is no city worth taking in that land now. He first tells us what will be done while the devil is confined. "And it shall be in that day that living waters shall go out from Jerusalem; half of them toward the former sea, and half of them toward the hinder sea; in summer and winter shall it be. And the Lord shall be king over all the earth; in that day shall there be one Lord, and his name one." There is living water and sea on the earth then, and it must be before the end of the world. "All the land shall be turned as a plain south of Jerusalem, and it shall be lifted up and inhabited in her place, from Benjamin's gate unto the place of the first gate, unto the corner gate, and from the tower of Hananeel unto the king's winepresses. And men shall dwell in it, and there shall be no more utter destruction, but Jerusalem shall be safely inhabited." (Zech. 14 : 8, 9, 10, 11.)

From this we learn that Jerusalem will be rebuilt, and will not be overthrown again until the end of the world. And then the new Jerusalem that will come down from heaven will take its place and stand forever. In the same chapter we are told what the Lord will do with an army that comes to make war on Jerusalem after the release of the devil: "And this shall be the plague wherewith the Lord will smite all the people that have fought against Jerusalem: their flesh shall consume away while they stand upon their feet, and their eyes shall consume away in their holes, and their tongue shall consume away in their mouth.

"And so shall be the plague of the horse, of the mule, of the camel, and of the ass, and of all the beasts that shall be in these tents, as this plague." (Zech. 14 : 12–15.) The verses following tell us what the Lord will do with the nations that will make war on Jerusalem if they do not go up to Jerusalem once a year to "worship the King, the Lord of hosts, and to keep the feast of tabernacles. And it shall be that whoso will not come up of all the families of the earth unto Jerusalem to worship the King, the Lord of hosts, even upon them shall be no rain. And if the family of Egypt go not up, and come not, that have no rain, there shall be the plague wherewith the Lord will smite the heathen that come not up to keep the feast of tabernacles. This shall be the punishment of Egypt, and the punishment of all nations that come not up to keep the feast of tabernacles. In that day shall there be upon the bells of the horses HOLINESS UNTO THE LORD, and the pots in the Lord's house shall be like the bowls before the altar. Yea, every pot in Jerusalem, and in Judah shall be holiness unto the Lord of hosts; and all they that sacrifice shall come and take of them, and seethe therein; and in that day there shall be no more the Canaanite in the house of the Lord of hosts." (Zech. 14 : 16, 17, 19, 20, 21.) The Lord is king in Jerusalem, then the devil is at liberty and is deceiving the nations of the earth, and the Lord deprives them of rain and sends a plague among them to make them worship him. The Lord will do this for their good, or afflict them to make them worship him and be saved.

The first two verses in this chapter were fulfilled in the overthrow of Jerusalem by the army gathered from the Roman Empire, and that army was from all nations then. If the first two verses had a literal fulfillment, what reason can we give for not believing the rest of the chapter will have? It tells us what will be done in Jerusalem after the crucifixion of Christ, and what will be done at his second coming, and what will be done after the devil is loosed for a season. It covers a long period of time in the world's history, and it gives us a key to unlock the book of prophecy by giving us a history of the different changes through which our fallen race must pass before and after the end of the world, or the end of our race in this human form. "I will bring forth my servant the BRANCH. For behold, the stone that I have laid before Joshua; upon one stone shall be seven eyes; behold, I will engrave the graving thereof, saith the Lord of hosts, and I will remove the iniquity of that land in one day. In that day, saith the Lord of hosts, shall ye call every man his neighbor under the vine and under the fig-tree." (Zech. 3 : 9, 10.)

That has not been fulfilled yet, but it will be, and cannot be at Christ's last coming, for then he comes to judge all who live on the earth then. "As a shepherd seeketh out his flock that are scattered, so will I seek out my sheep, and will deliver them out of all places where they have been scattered in the cloudy and dark days. (The Jews have had many cloudy days since Christ's first coming.) And I will bring them out from the people and gather them from the countries, and will bring them to their own land, and feed them upon the mountains of Israel, by the rivers, and in all the inhabited places of the country. I will feed them in good pasture upon the high mountains of Israel. I will feed my flock, and I will cause them to lie down, saith the Lord God. I will seek that which was lost, and bring again that which was driven away; and I will bind up that which was sick. Therefore will I save my flock, and they shall no more be a prey. And I will set up one shepherd over them, and he shall feed them, even my servant David; he shall feed them, and he shall be their shepherd." (Ezek. 34 : 12–23.) The Lord has scattered his people, and he has promised to bring them from among the people and feed them on the mountains of Israel, and in all the inhabited places of that country; and David may have part in the first resurrection, and he may feed them or help rule over them while Satan is bound, or it may refer to Christ. This does not refer to the Jews in heaven coming back in a spiritual body on a re-created earth; and it does not refer to taking the Jews from the earth to heaven, for he brings them from the countries in which he has scattered them and takes them to the land of Israel. And it does not refer to a spiritual birth of the soul, for "thus, saith the Lord of hosts, Again in this place, which is desolate without man and without beast, and in all the cities thereof shall be a habitation of shepherds causing their flocks to lie down. In the cities of the mountains, in the cities of the vale, and in the cities of the south, and in the land of Benjamin, and in the places about Jerusalem, and in the cities of Judah, shall the flocks pass again under the hands of him that telleth them, saith the Lord. Behold, the days come, saith the Lord, that I will perform that good thing which I have promised unto the house of Israel, and to the house of Judah. In those days, and at that time, will I cause the branch of righteousness to grow up unto David; and he shall execute judgment and righteousness in the land." That branch is Christ at his second coming. "In those days shall Judah be saved, and Jerusalem shall dwell safely; and this is the name wherewith she shall be called, THE LORD OUR RIGHTEOUSNESS. For thus saith the Lord, David shall never want a man to sit upon the throne of the house of Israel." (Jer. 33 : 12–17.) Christ will then commence his reign as a king.

And this could not be done on a re-created earth or world. For we are not told that the animal creation will be raised from the dead and given a spiritual body and live forever on a new earth. This

"Branch of Righteousness" that shall execute judgment in Jerusalem at that time is Christ. And the prophet is telling us what will be in that country at that time. And he has told us there will be shepherds causing their flocks to lie down in all that country, that has been barren for a long time. And Christ said, "I will perform that good thing which I have promised to the house of Israel, and to the house of Judah." It is not promised to all nations on the earth, but is confined to the land the Lord gave to the descendants of Abraham, and does not include all the earth. But the earth will all be inhabited then, for the nations of the earth at that time will come to Jerusalem to worship the Lord of Hosts. "At the same time, saith the Lord, will I be the God of all the families of Israel, and they shall be my people. The Lord hath appeared of old unto me, saying, Yea, I have loved thee with an everlasting love: therefore with lovingkindness have I drawn thee. Again I will build thee, and thou shalt be built: O virgin of Israel, thou shalt again be adorned with thy tabrets, and shalt go forth in the dances of them that make merry." This is not in heaven, for he said, "Thou shalt yet plant vines upon the mountains of Samaria; the planters shall plant, and shall eat them as common things. For there shall be a day that the watchman upon the Mount Ephraim shall cry, Arise ye, and let us go up to Zion unto the Lord our God. For thus saith the Lord: Sing with gladness for Jacob, and shout among the chief of the nations; publish ye, praise ye, and say, O Lord, save thy people, the remnant of Israel! Behold, I will bring them from the north country, and gather them from the coasts of the earth, and with them the blind and the lame, the woman with child and her that travaileth with child together: a great company shall return thither. They shall come with weeping, and with supplications will I lead them: I will cause them to walk by the rivers of waters in a strait way wherein they shall not stumble: for I am a father to Israel, and Ephraim is my first-born. Hear the word of the Lord, O ye nations, and declare it in the isles afar off, and say, He that scattereth Israel will gather him, and keep him, as a shepherd doth his flock. For the Lord hath redeemed Jacob, and ransomed him from the hand of him that was stronger than he (meaning the evil spirit). Therefore they shall come and sing in the height of Zion, and shall flow together to the goodness of the Lord, for wheat, and for wine, and for oil, and for the young of the flock and of the herd; and their soul shall be as a watered garden; and they shall not sorrow any more at all. Then shall the virgin rejoice in the dance, both young men and old together: for I will turn their mourning into joy, and I will comfort them, and make them rejoice from their sorrow." (Jer. 31 : 1–13.)

This promise is made to the Jews by the Lord of hosts. It has not been fulfilled yet, and it could not be fulfilled after the end of the world; but it will be fulfilled while the devil is confined and Christ is King over the earth. Men are in a body of flesh and blood then; the virgin, young men, and old men will rejoice together in the dance. And how can all nations declare it to the isles of the sea while they refuse to believe it? And thus saith the Lord to Israel, "I will gather the remnant of my flock out of all countries whither I have driven them, and will bring them again to their folds: and they shall be fruitful and increase (not in heaven); and I will set up shepherds over them which shall feed them: and they shall fear no more, nor be dismayed, neither shall they be lacking, saith the Lord. Behold, the days come, saith the Lord, that I will raise unto David a righteous branch, and a king shall reign and prosper, and shall execute judgment and justice in the earth. In his days Judah shall be saved, and Israel shall dwell safely: and this is his name whereby he shall be called, THE LORD OUR RIGHTEOUSNESS. Therefore, behold, the days come, saith the Lord, that they shall no more say, The Lord liveth which brought up the children of Israel out of the land of Egypt; but, The Lord liveth which brought up and which led the seed of the house of Israel out of the north country, and from all countries whither I had driven them; and they shall dwell in their own land." (Jer. 23 : 3–8.)

Their deliverance from Egypt did fulfill prophecy; and to fulfill prophecy they must return to their own land, and worship the God of their fathers, and believe on his Son. I do not see how we can misunderstand this prophecy. For the Lord has promised to gather his people Israel from all the countries in which they are scattered, to the land he gave to their fathers. And Christ is to be a King in the place of David in Judah, and he shall reign and prosper and execute judgment. This is not in heaven, or on a new earth, and it must be done before the end of the world and the last resurrection. "Rejoice ye with Jerusalem, and be glad with her, all ye that love her: rejoice for joy with her, all ye that mourn for her. For thus saith the Lord, Behold, I will extend peace to her like a river, and the glory of the Gentiles like a flowing stream: then shall ye suck, ye shall be borne upon her sides, and be dandled upon her knees. As one whom his mother comforteth, so will I comfort you: and ye shall be comforted in Jerusalem." (Isa. 66 : 10, 12, 13.)

The Jews have not been comforted in Jerusalem since the death and resurrection of Christ. How can they be a nation without a king? The Lord has promised to send them a king from heaven, and told them his name. The Jews believe Christ will come to be a king; what reason can we give for not believing it? "Therefore thus saith the Lord God: Now will I bring again the captivity of Jacob, and have mercy upon the whole house of Israel, and will be jealous for my holy name. After they have borne their shame, and all their trespasses whereby they have trespassed against me." They are doing that now. And then, "When I have brought them again from the people, and gathered them out of their enemies' land, and am sanctified in them in the sight of many nations, then shall they know that I am the Lord their God, which caused them to be led into captivity among the heathen; but I have gathered them up into their own land, and have left none of them any more there. Neither will I hide my face any more from them, for I have poured out my spirit upon the house of Israel, saith the Lord God." (Ezek. 39 : 25–29.)

The Lord speaks to us again, saying, "Behold I have given him for a witness to the people, a leader and commander to the people. For ye shall go out with joy, and be led forth with peace; the mountains and the hills shall break forth before you into singing, and all the trees of the field shall clap their hands. Instead of the thorn shall come up the fir-tree, and instead of the brier shall come up the myrtle-tree, and it shall be to the Lord for a name, for an everlasting sign, that shall not be cut off." (Isa. 55 : 4, 12, 13.) The Lord will come to be a leader and commander to his people, and the devil will be confined and sealed up in the bottomless pit; and then the earth will not bring forth the thorn and the brier, for the curse is removed till the devil is released again. And all nations will praise the Lord for removing from the earth, for a time, sin and its curse. So the men who live then can see what sin has cost Adam's race. And the Jews will not forget what the Lord has done for them, and what he will teach them, when the devil is confined and Christ is their king ; they will remember it to the end of the world, and then the devil will be confined forever.

"Thus saith the Lord God, Behold I will take the children of Israel from among the heathen, whither they be gone, and will gather them on every side, and bring them into their own land. And I will make them one nation in the land upon the mountains of Israel ; and one king shall be king to them all, and they shall be no more two nations, neither shall they be divided into two kingdoms any more at all. Neither shall they defile themselves any more with their idols, nor with their detestable things nor with any of their transgressions ; but I will save them out of all their dwelling-places wherein they have sinned, and will cleanse them, so shall they be my people, and I will be their God. And David my servant shall be king over them ; and they all shall have one shepherd." They had been two nations from Solomon's death to Christ; and no nation since that time. "They shall also walk in my judgments and observe my statues, and do them." They have not done that. "And they shall dwell in the land that I have given unto Jacob my servant, wherein your fathers have dwelt, and they shall dwell therein, even they, and their children, and their children's children forever ; and my servant David shall be their prince forever." This will begin at Christ's second coming, who is typified under the name of

David. "I will make a covenant of peace with them; it shall be an everlasting covenant with them; and I will place them and multiply them, and will set my sanctuary in the midst of them forevermore." And again thus saith the Lord: "My tabernacle also shall be with them, yea, I will be their God, and they shall be my people. And the heathen shall know that I the Lord do sanctify Israel, when my sanctuary shall be in the midst of them forevermore." (Ezek. 37: 21-28.)

The Lord has told us in this that he will restore Israel to their native land forever, but he does it while they have children, and while the heathen nations are round about them; and they will dwell in the land the Lord promised to Abraham and his seed, for an everlasting possession. This will be done many years before the end comes, and the race of Adam ceases to multiply on the earth. "Behold, I will gather them out of all countries whither I have driven them in mine anger, and in my fury, and in great wrath; and I will bring them again unto this place; and I will cause them to dwell safely. And they shall be my people, and I will be their God. And I will give them one heart, and one way, that they may fear me forever, for the good of them, and of their children after them. And I will make an everlasting covenant with them to do them good; but I will put my fear in their hearts, that they shall not depart from me, yea, I will rejoice over them to do them good, and I will plant them in this land assuredly with my whole heart, and with my whole soul. For thus saith the Lord, Like as I have brought all this great evil upon this people, so will I bring upon them all the good that I have promised them." (Jer. 32 : 37–42.) Why not believe this? For, "Behold, the days come, saith the Lord, that I will make a new covenant with the house of Israel, and with the house of Judah." And the Lord will do it for all who live at that time. "Not according to the covenant that I made with their fathers in the day that I took them by the hand to bring them out of the land of Egypt, which my covenant they brake, although I was a husband unto them, saith the Lord. But this shall be the covenant that I will make with the house of Israel after those days, saith the Lord: I will put my law in their inward parts, and write it in their hearts, and will be their God, and they shall be my people (the Lord has not done this yet), and they shall teach no more every man his neighbor, and every man his brother, saying, Know the Lord, for they shall all know me, from the least of them unto the greatest of them, saith the Lord, for I will forgive their iniquity, and I will remember their sin no more." (Jer. 31 : 31–34.)

This promise has not been fulfilled to the Jewish nation. This new covenant was offered them by Christ when he first came, to instruct and bless them. They would not receive him, or his Spirit, or the new covenant, or new birth, and have not yet. But when they do receive it, as it is promised, they will all receive it, from the least to the greatest of them, for all shall know the Lord, and be by him forgiven, and he will remember their sin no more. Preaching Christ's gospel will never do this while the devil is at liberty to deceive them; but when the devil is sealed up in the bottomless pit for a thousand years; and when Christ comes to be a king over them—as he has promised he would be—they will receive him, believe on him, and receive the blessing he has promised them in this life as a nation, and all he has promised in a future state. They are not offering the sacrifice offered by their fathers, or receiving and believing on the sacrifice made by Christ for them, for they have not complied with the conditions demanded by Christ, before he could forgive their sins, give them his Spirit, and write his law in their hearts, and they receive his new covenant. Not according to the covenant he made with their fathers, for they did not obey that law or keep that covenant, and they are not doing it to this day. They are not keeping the old or new covenant now, and have not since Christ's death; again: "And speak unto him, saying, Thus speaketh the Lord of hosts, saying, Behold the man whose name is THE BRANCH; and he shall grow up out of his place, and he shall build the temple of the Lord. Even he shall build the temple of the Lord, and he shall bear the glory, and shall sit and rule upon his throne, and he shall be a priest upon his throne; and the counsel of peace shall be between them both." (Zech. 6 : 12, 13.)

This prophecy does not refer to their return from Babylon, for they had not been driven in all countries then; and the Lord did not give them one heart and one way then, and their children after them, and the covenant he made with them then, he did not call an everlasting covenant, and he did not put his fear into their hearts and he has not put his fear in the hearts of their children after them, and the Lord did not bring on them all the good he has promised them, and the Lord told them that they broke the covenant he made with their fathers, and he had been a husband to them, and the new covenant he promised to make with them was to put his law in their inward parts, and write it in their hearts, and he will be their God, and they shall be his people. The Lord has not done that for them yet, and they do not all know the Lord yet; but they will at Christ's second coming. Then the prophet calls Christ the man, and his name is THE BRANCH, he will grow up out of his place, and he shall build the temple of the Lord, and he shall rule on his throne; and the counsel of peace shall be between them both (him and his people). "And I will rebuke the devourer for your sakes, and he shall not destroy the fruits of your ground; neither shall your vines cast her fruit before the time in the field, saith the Lord of hosts; and all nations shall call you blessed; for ye shall be a delightsome land, saith the Lord of hosts." (Mal. 3 : 11, 12.)

That prophecy was written 397 years before Christ's

first coming, and it has not been fulfilled yet; and all prophecy must be fulfilled, and the Jews had no prophet from that time till Christ came. Again he has said: "In that day shall the Lord defend the inhabitants of Jerusalem; and he that is feeble among them at that day shall be as David; and the house of David shall be as God, as the angel of the Lord, before them. And it shall come to pass in that day that I will seek to destroy all the nations that come against Jerusalem. And I will pour upon the house of David, and upon the inhabitants of Jerusalem, the spirit of grace and of supplications; and they shall look upon me whom they have pierced, and they shall mourn for him as one mourneth for his only son, and shall be in bitterness for him as one that is in bitterness for his first born. In that day shall there be a great mourning in Jerusalem." (Zech. 12 : 8–11.) In that day Christ will belong to the house of David and will be as God, and David as the angel of the Lord. In that day sin remains on the earth, for the Lord will destroy all the nations that come against Jerusalem. And the Jews will mourn when they look on Christ, and know that their fathers did pierce and crucify the son of God. "And I will strengthen the house of Judah, and I will save the house of Joseph, and I will bring them again to place them, for I have mercy upon them, and they shall be as though I had not cast them off, for I am the Lord their God, and will hear them. I will hiss for them, and gather them, for I have redeemed them, and they shall increase as they have increased. I will bring them again also out of the land of Egypt, and gather them out of Assyria, and I will bring them into the land of Gilead and Lebanon, and place shall not be found for them." (Zech. 10 : 6, 8, 10.) "Another angel said unto him, Run, speak to this young man, saying, Jerusalem shall be inhabited as towns without walls for the multitude of men and cattle therein. Deliver thyself, O Zion, that dwellest with the daughter of Babylon."

That has not been done in Jerusalem yet, but it must be before the end comes, for they have cattle and a multitude of men, not like angels, as they will be in the new creation. "For thus saith the Lord of hosts : After the glory hath he sent me unto the nations which spoiled you, for he that toucheth you toucheth the apple of his eye. For, behold I will shake my hand upon them, and they shall be a spoil to their servants; and ye shall know that the Lord of hosts has sent me." That "ME" means Christ. "Sing and rejoice, O daughter of Zion, for lo, I come, and I will dwell in the midst of thee, saith the Lord. And many nations shall be joined to the Lord in that day, and shall be my people. And the Lord shall inherit Judah, his portion in the holy land, and shall choose Jerusalem again. Be silent, O all flesh, before the Lord, for he is raised up out of his holy habitation." (Zech. 2 : 4-13.) The son of God is telling the Jews what he will do for them in the latter days on the earth, and he has not done this good thing for them in Jerusalem yet. His call is to all of the Jews, and he tells them he will come and dwell in the midst of them, and deliver them from the power of the devil, and from all the nations in which he has scattered them. "For thus saith the Lord of hosts: Yet once it is a little while, and I will shake the heavens, and the earth, and the sea, and the dry land. And I will shake all nations, and the desire of all nations shall come; and I will fill this house with glory, saith the Lord of hosts. The silver is mine, and the gold is mine, saith the Lord of hosts. The glory of this latter house shall be greater than of the former, saith the Lord of hosts, and in this place will I give peace, saith the Lord of hosts." (Hag. 2 : 6-9.)

The Lord will build another temple in the place of the one that was thrown down. But it is not the temple that will come down from heaven at Christ's third coming to make all things new. For the silver and gold are his, and he will use it in building the temple he has been telling us about, and calls it a house that he will fill with his glory, and he will give his peace to that place. That could not be done at Christ's last coming; but it will all be done at his second coming. That prophecy was written five hundred and twenty years before Christ, and it was not done in the temple then standing. "Then thou shalt see, and flow together, and thine heart shall fear and be enlarged; because the abundance of the sea shall be converted unto thee, the forces of the

Gentiles shall come unto thee. All the flocks of Kedar shall be gathered together unto thee, the rams of Nebaioth shall minister unto thee; they shall come up with acceptance on mine altar, and I will glorify the house of my glory. Who are these that fly as a cloud, and as the doves to their windows? Surely the isles shall wait for me, and the ships of Tarshish first, to bring thy sons from far, their silver and their gold with them, unto the name of the Lord thy God, and to the Holy One of Israel because he hath glorified thee. And the sons of strangers shall build up thy walls, and their kings shall minister unto thee: for in my wrath I smote thee, but in my favor have I had mercy on thee. Therefore thy gates shall be open continually: they shall not be shut day nor night, that men may bring unto thee the forces of the Gentiles, and that their kings may be brought." The prophet calls them men, not angels, or men with a spiritual body. "For the nation and kingdom that will not serve thee shall perish; yea, those nations shall be utterly wasted. The glory of Lebanon shall come unto thee, the fir-tree, the pine-tree, and the box together, to beautify the place of my sanctuary; and I will make the place of my feet glorious. The sons also of them that afflicted thee shall come bending unto thee; and all they that despised thee shall bow themselves down at the soles of thy feet; and they shall call thee, The city of the Lord, The Zion of the Holy One of Israel." (Isa. 60 : 5–14.)

This will all be done in Jerusalem at the SECOND COMING OF CHRIST. When the devil is confined and all nations will be converted to Christ, Jerusalem and the temple will be built up, and the sons of strangers will help do it, and all nations and kings will serve them, for the Lord will be king over them, the Holy One of Israel. "And there shall come forth a rod out of the stem of Jesse, and a BRANCH shall grow out of his roots. And Righteousness shall be the girdle of his loins, and Faithfulness the girdle of his reins. The wolf also shall dwell with the lamb, and the leopard shall lie down with the kid, and the calf and the young lion and the fatling together, and a little child shall lead them. And the cow and the bear shall feed, their young ones shall lie down together; and the lion shall eat straw like the ox. And the sucking child shall play on the hole of the asp, and the weaned child shall put his hand on the cockatrice's den. They shall not hurt nor destroy in all my holy mountain; for the earth shall be full of the knowledge of the Lord as the waters cover the sea. And in that day there shall be a root of Jesse, which shall stand for an ensign of the people; to it shall the Gentiles seek; and his rest shall be glorious." (Isa. 11 : 1, 5, 6, 7, 8, 9, 10.)

The gospel and spirit of Christ have made a great change in some men. But it has not changed the nature of the lion, wolf, and leopard. The only way to make all that live on the earth good is to remove from the earth the author of all that is evil. The devil is the author of all that is evil in man and in all the animal creation. And the devil is the enemy who sowed the tares in the wheat. When Adam obeyed Satan the ground did bring forth thorns and thistles; and from the fall of Adam to the present time the earth, and all who live on it, have been controlled more or less by the devil, the author of all evil. Then if the old serpent, or Satan, was sealed up in a bottomless pit so he could not deceive and control anything that lives on the earth for a thousand years, then there could be no evil on the earth. When the legion of devils went out of the man who lived in the mountains and in the tombs, he was clothed and in his right mind. Jesus made the change in that man, and he can make the change in all created things in the same way; and the Lord will do it, for he has told the prophets to tell us he would do it. And at that time he will make the same change in men who live on the earth, and this must all be done before the end of the world. He did not at his first coming free the Jews from the control of the evil spirit as a nation; he has not done it yet. But Paul has told us, "All Israel shall be saved." (Rom. 11 : 26.) He did not intend for us to understand that all the Jews who lived then, and all who would live from that time to Christ's second coming, would be saved. But all who live on the earth when he comes to confine the author of sin, they shall and will all be saved. That is the only way we can explain Paul's statement. Deprive the evil spirit of the power he has to control and deceive men, and blindness will depart from Israel. "Shall the earth be made to bring forth in one day, or shall a nation be born at once?" (Isa. 66 : 8.) This will be done. Remove the cause of evil, and you will remove the power sin has over men and all creation. And we are told that Christ will "set up an ensign for the nations, and shall assemble the outcasts of Israel, and gather together the dispersed of Judah from the four corners of the earth. The envy also of Ephraim shall depart, and the adversaries of Judah shall be cut off. Ephraim shall not envy Judah, and Judah shall not vex Ephraim." (Isa. 11 : 12, 13.)

This has not been done and will not be done until the author of that envy is removed from the minds of men. The Lord has promised to do it, and he will do it even if all men refuse to believe it. Is anything too hard for the Lord? We answer, No. And all this must be done before the end of the world, for then the devil will be confined forever.

"The wolf and the lamb shall feed together, and the lion shall eat straw like the bullock, and the dust shall be the serpent's meat. They shall not hurt nor destroy in all my holy mountain, saith the Lord." (Isa. 65 : 25.) "And they shall bring all your brethren for an offering unto the Lord out of all nations, upon horses, and in chariots, and in litters, and upon mules, and upon swift beasts, to my holy mountain Jerusalem, saith the Lord, as the children of Israel bring an offering in a clean vessel into the house of the Lord." (Isa. 66 : 20.) Men in a spiritual body after the last resurrection will not be taken to Jerusalem in that way. Christ at his first coming did every little thing the prophets had said he would do. Can he overlook all this at his second coming? The fulfillment of prophecy in the past proves that all the rest of God's promises will be fulfilled. "And he said unto Abram, Know, of a surety, that thy seed shall be a stranger in a land that is not theirs, and shall serve them; and they shall afflict them four hundred years. And also that nation whom they shall serve will I judge; and afterward shall they come out with great substance." (Gen. 15 : 13, 14.)

This had a literal fulfillment, and when we read the account given of its fulfillment, we must admit the Lord is faithful to do all he has promised, and terrible in the execution of his judgments. "Now the Lord had said unto Abram, Get thee out of thy country, and from thy kindred, and from thy father's house, unto a land that I will shew thee; and I will make thee a great nation, and I will bless thee, and make thy name great; and thou shalt be a blessing; and I will bless them that bless thee, and curse him that curseth thee, and in thee shall all families of the earth be blessed." (Gen. 12 : 1-3.) This promise was made to Abram 3,810 years ago; the promise is to those who live on the earth at Christ's second coming, and not to the dead; and all the families of the earth have not been blessed in Christ or in

Abram yet, but they will be when the devil is bound and sealed up in prison for a thousand years. All those living at that time will be blessed by Christ at his second coming, in this life, and in a future state. "In that day shall this song be sung in the land of Judah: We have a strong city; salvation will God appoint for walls and bulwarks. Open ye the gates, that the righteous nation which keepeth the truth may enter in." (Isa. 26 : 1, 2.) After the devil is loosed for a season there will be unrighteous nations that will not be permitted to come into Jerusalem, and they will make war on the city; but they will not take it, for that city and nation will fear the Lord, and be protected by him, from the restoration to the end of the world. "And in that day will I make a covenant for them with the beasts of the field, and with the fowls of heaven, and with the creeping things of the ground; and I will break the bow and the sword and the battle out of the earth, and I will make them to lie down safely." (Hos. 2 : 18.) While the devil is confined the wild beasts will harm no one, and all can lie down safely.

Peter in his sermon to the Jews said: "David was a prophet, and knowing that God had sworn with an oath to him that of the fruit of his loins, according to the flesh, he would raise up Christ to sit on his throne, he, seeing this before, spake of the resurrection of Christ, that his soul was not left in hell, neither his flesh did see corruption." (Acts 2 : 30, 31.) Christ's body was not left in the grave, and his soul was not left on or in this earth, the devil's home, for he went to paradise, returned to the earth, raised his body from the grave, and then ascended to his Father; and he has not been a king on David's throne yet, but at his second coming he will be. "When the fullness of the Gentiles comes in, all Israel shall be saved; as it is written: There shall come out of Zion the Deliverer, and shall turn away ungodliness from Jacob. For this is my covenant unto them, when I shall take away their sins." (Rom. 11 : 26, 27.) The Lord has not taken away their sins yet, but he will take away the sins of all who live at his next coming. "But this man, after he had offered one sacrifice for sin forever, sat down on the right hand of God. From henceforth expecting till his enemies be made his footstool." (Heb. 10 : 12, 13.) The Lord is willing to forgive sin, and baptize us with the Holy Spirit. But he wants men willing to receive it and obey his commands. The Jews have not believed on him or been willing to receive him yet. "But they shall serve the Lord their God and David their king, whom I will raise up unto them. Fear not, O my servant Jacob, saith the Lord; neither be dismayed, O Israel; for lo, I will save thee from afar, and thy seed from the land of their captivity; and Jacob shall return, and shall be in rest, and be quiet, and none shall make him afraid." (Jer. 30 : 9, 10.) Israel has not returned to the Lord, and he has not raised up David their king, and Christ has not been king on David's throne in Jerusalem. But all this must be done, for the Lord of hosts has spoken it.

"Jesus said to Peter, If I will that he tarry till I come, what is that to thee?" By this Jesus would have us understand that John would die a natural death, or that he would live till Christ, the giver of life, came to take him from this earthly tabernacle to occupy a spiritual body in a future state; other passages in the New Testament that speak of the coming of Christ can be construed in the same way. He came to Saul, and asked him why he persecuted him, and he freed Saul from the control of Satan. "Be ye also ready for in such an hour as ye think not, the Son of man cometh." (Matt. 24 : 44.) Our death ends our personal interest in this world, or in God's promises to us, unless they refer to Christ's third coming to raise the dead and make all things new. That would divide what is said in the Bible, about Christ's coming, in four parts; and if the readers of the Bible would keep that in mind it would help them to understand what coming is spoken of, and whether it has or has not been fulfilled. All Christ has promised to do on the earth before the end comes will be done, and if all the nations of the earth should oppose it they would be like the kings of Egypt and Babylon; when they are weighed in God's balance they will be found wanting, for Christ has said: "Except ye repent, ye shall all likewise perish." (Luke 13 : 5.) It is wisdom to believe God's promises, obey his commands, submit to the dispensations of his Providence, and say, "Thy will be done," for "thou doest all things well;" for he does not afflict willingly, and those light afflictions will, if received in the right spirit "work out for us a far more exceeding and eternal weight of glory," that will be given to us by Christ, the Judge of all the earth, when our work for him is done and our mortal life is ended. For his power to save is unbounded; our work in his vineyard will soon end, and the reward is at the end of the race. We may not live on the earth to see all this fulfilled, but our descendants will see and know it has all been done, and well done, and they can tell us all about it in heaven, or on a recreated earth.

Christ at his second coming will not go into Egypt to escape from Herod or the kings of the earth, for they will put up their swords and cast their crowns at his feet, and hail him as "Lord of lords, and King of kings." For then he comes to bring peace and good-will to men and to all the brute creation, and all will say, "Lord, what wilt thou have me to do?" For he will be king over all the earth for a thousand years, with none to dispute his power. For the devil, the enemy of God and man, will be sealed up in the bottomless pit or in this earth. This covenant of peace will be made with all men who live on the earth at that time. And it will be made with the evil beasts in the wilderness. "And I will make with them a covenant of peace, and will cause the evil beasts to cease out of the land; and they shall dwell safely in the wilderness and sleep in the woods." (Ezek. 34 : 25.) That covenant has never been made. And there will be no evil beasts, and men will not sleep in the woods in heaven, and they will not on a re-created earth. But when the devil is sealed up in the earth the lion and the wolf will not harm the lamb. "And I will make them and the places round about my hill a blessing; and I will cause the shower to come down in his season: there shall be showers of blessings. And the tree of the field shall yield her fruit, and the earth shall yield her increase, and they shall dwell safe in their land." (Ezek. 34 : 26, 27.) This follows the verse quoted above. And it could not be on a renovated earth, for on that there will be no more sea. There would be no showers to come down. And the trees of the field would not yield her fruit, or the earth her increase. And it could not be in heaven. It will be on the earth while the devil is confined in the earth. It is the evil spirit who makes the serpent and the evil beasts the enemies of man, and it is that spirit who makes man his own enemy. That spirit does not want men to believe the Bible, or obey the commands of their Creator. The devil offered Christ the kingdoms of this world, and the Jews wanted him to be a king. He would not take the sceptre from them, but he will take it from his Father, and then he will confine the devil who tried to deceive him. He will be a king then with no rival or a peer, and all who read this book will understand and believe this if the devil does not blind them. It will not pay men to be blinded by him. The past history of God's dealings with men proves this, and proves that the evil spirit is the author of deception and all the changes men have made in the Word of God. God is a God of mercy, and the past proves he is a God of justice and judgment.

The prophets have told us what Christ will do, but they have not told us when he will do it. And we know he has not done all they have said he would do, but he will do it. For Paul, after Christ's first coming, has told us, "He shall appear the second time without sin unto salvation." (Heb. 9 : 28.) And we are told Christ will "cast out the old serpent, called the devil and Satan, which deceiveth the whole world; he was cast out into the earth, and his angels were cast out with him. Then is come salvation, and strength, and the kingdom of our God, and the power of his Christ." (Rev. 12 : 9, 10.) He has not deprived the devil of his power yet; but we are told he will come and confine the devil and his angels one thousand years, and then they will be loosed for a season, and at the end of that time, called "a little season," the devil is to be cast into the lake of fire and brimstone for ever and ever. (Rev. 20.) This is told us after Christ's first coming. And what he did and permitted men to do to him then are the hardest things we are asked to believe the Creator of the world would do or permit men to do to him. We believe Christ appeared to men on the earth from the creation to the days of Abraham. And we should believe he will come and confine the devil, and bring salvation to all who live on the earth while he is confined, for it has all been written by the same prophets. Paul has told us in 1 Cor. 15 what Christ will do at his last coming. He does not bring salvation then, for he ends the multiplication of Adam's race.

Christ has told us to pray for "Thy kingdom to come. Thy will be done on earth as it is in heaven." (Matt. 6 : 10.) That prayer is for Christ's second coming, for he is not a king over all men yet. There is a good deal of the devil's will done, and he has not given up the kingdom to Christ. And Paul has told us, " The God of peace shall bruise Satan under our feet shortly." (Rom. 16 : 20.) And Christ has not come to the earth yet as a " God of peace," and he has not bruised Satan under our feet. But at his second coming to bring salvation to all who live on the earth at that time he will be a God of peace, and he will bruise Satan under their feet. When he seals him up in the bottomless pit in this earth he will be under the feet of all men who are then on the earth. Then he " will break the bow and the sword and the battle out of the earth, and will make them to lie down safely, and I will say to them which were not my people, Thou art my people, and they shall say, Thou art my God." (Hos. 2 : 18–23.) This could not be done at his last coming, for then all who live on the earth must die, and all who are not his people then never will be. I do not understand how the devil can make men believe that all unfulfilled prophecy can be fulfilled at Christ's last coming, or in heaven, or on a renovated earth, for prophecy is not given to instruct men after they leave this sinful world.

1. This life, to many, will compare
    With what we call a dream;
   Its sleep, or blindness, hides from them
    The future that *could* be seen.

2. For faith in what has been revealed
    From heaven's eternal light,
   Would let us see the future world
    Through this life's darkest night.

3. Christ's second coming will unfold
    To all who then live on earth,
   What in the thousand years will be;
    What Christ's birth and death are worth.

4. Then Satan will be loosed again
    From his prison, to go free
   To deceive our race for ages,
    Before the end will be.

5. Then the old serpent and his work
    Will forever be confined;
   If we believe what is revealed
    This could not be denied.

CHRIST'S THIRD COMING.

THE THIRD COMING OF CHRIST TO BE THE LION OF THE TRIBE OF JUDAH will be to judge the world at the last resurrection, to confine death, the devil and all his works, in a "lake of fire forever." This is called the second coming of Christ, WHICH IS A MISTAKE, and it has blinded the Gentile Churches so they do not believe what is said about his SECOND COMING, to fulfill prophecy he could not fulfill at this coming; and they have misunderstood what is meant by the first resurrection "of them who were beheaded for the witness of Jesus and for the Word of God, and they lived and reigned with Christ a thousand years." (Rev. 20 : 4.) If *men* have taught us erroneously to mix the second and third coming of Christ together, it is our duty to separate them, for all who have been put to death for believing God's Word will reign with Christ forever in heaven.

The prophets are not referring to that, for they speak of a reign with Christ for a thousand years on the earth. They come from heaven to the earth, are raised from the dead, and Christ must come with them, or they could not reign with him. And the Prophet tells us at that time an angel will confine the old serpent, which is the devil and Satan, a thousand years. This is not forever, and is a work done for the race of Adam, who live on the earth at that time. And Christ will bring a few from heaven to reign with him, or help him rule over the nations of the earth, while the devil is confined for a thousand years. And then the devil is loosed from his prison to deceive the nations of the earth. The above shows he could not have deceived them in the thousand years he had been confined ; and at Christ's last coming in judgment the devil is to be confined forever. We learn from this that Christ did not do all he has promised to do at his first and second coming, and all prophecy must be fulfilled. So let us see what the prophets say about Christ's third or last coming in the history of Adam's race, while they live in a human body on this earth before it is re-created. Those who live on the earth then will or " shall see the Son of man coming in the clouds of heaven, with power and great glory. And he shall send his angels with a great sound of a trumpet, and they shall gather together his elect from the four winds, from one end of heaven to the other." (Matt. 24 : 30, 31.) " This generation (or the race of Adam) shall not pass till all these things be fulfilled. Heaven and earth shall pass away, but my words shall not pass away." (Matt. 24 : 34, 35.) The earth and the air as it is will pass away or be changed, but it will not be consumed, for the earth will stand forever. Mark, in his Gospel, speaks of this event, and uses nearly the same language. That event will be the end of Adam's race in a human form, and the end of sin on the earth forever.

We will now look at some things that will come to pass before the end comes; and we will see the third coming is a long way off if we view time from a human standpoint. The reader will remember that in referring to the second coming of Christ I have briefly referred to what the prophets have told us the Lord will do for the Jews "when the times of the Gentiles be fulfilled" (Luke. 21 : 24), which is to be followed by the second coming of Christ to confine the devil, who has and will till that time oppose the spread of the true Gospel of Christ, and then " The knowledge of the Lord will cover the earth as the waters cover the sea" (Isa. 11 : 9), " and one cannot say to the other, Know the Lord, for all shall know him, from the least unto the greatest of them, saith the Lord." (Jer. 31 : 34.) I have quoted this before, and I do it again, hoping the reader will stop and think what will be done for the human race on the earth in that time. Think how men will multiply on the earth, and that all the increase in that time will be prepared for Christ's kingdom in heaven! and the Prophet, referring to this increase, has told us, " The number of the children of Israel shall be as the sand of the sea, which cannot be measured nor numbered ; and it shall come to pass that in the place where it was said unto them, Ye are not my people, there it shall be said unto them, Ye are the sons of the living God." (Hos. 1 : 10.) And in the closing chapter of this prophecy he thus writes : " I will heal their backsliding, I will love them freely, for mine anger is turned away from him; I will be as the dew unto Israel ; he shall grow as the lily, and cast forth his roots as Lebanon ; his branches shall spread, and his beauty shall be as the olive-tree, and his smell as Lebanon. They that dwell under his shadow shall return; they shall revive as the corn, and grow as the vine; the scent thereof shall be as the wine of Lebanon." (Hos. 14 : 4-7.) That could not be fulfilled in this dispensation, but it will in the next, and the men who live in that time will be strangers to the devil and his works.

Christ has not told us he would leave men, after he had subdued the nations of the earth to himself. But if he did not leave the earth he would not have told us he would descend from heaven with his angels and all the saints. And he has told us the " devil will be loosed for a season " to deceive the nations of the earth. And we learn from this that confinement will not improve him. And the sinless race of Adam, then on the earth, will not be able to resist him, but they will do some things he tells them to do, and in that way become his servants; and as one step in sin prepares the way for another, Satan's followers will multiply, for it will be then, as it is now, easier to persuade men to do wrong than it is to do right. Men will make swords and spears, and make war on their fellow-men. One large army, we are told, will be consumed by fire from heaven. This large army had been deceived by Satan, and they had come from the four quarters of the earth, "to gather them together to battle; the number is as the sand of the sea. And they compassed the camp of the saints about, and the beloved city, and fire came down from God out of heaven and devoured them." (Rev. 20 : 8, 9.) There is no beloved city now. This could not be the new Jerusalem on a re-created earth. It is the result of the spread of sin after the release of Satan out of his prison, and before the third coming of Christ. All that is said about war, the plague, and the command of the Lord, saying, "that all nations must come up to Jerusalem and keep the feast of tabernacles, or they will be smitten with a plague and have no rain" (Zech. 15), will be fulfilled in that period of the world's history.

We have a short account of the fall of man and the spread of sin in the world, but it took two thousand years to prepare them for the flood. And we have a short account of the spread of sin after the release of the devil, and it may take two thousand years for the evil spirits to prepare men for the terrible plagues and judgments that John tells us the Lord will send on the earth to punish men, before the third or final coming of Christ, to deprive the devil of his power to deceive men on the earth forever. He will make the nations on the re-created earth like the angels in heaven, and they will not marry or be given in marriage, or increase on the earth after the third coming of Christ and the last resurrection. And all prophecy must be fulfilled then, and if we believe half the prophets tell us and refuse to believe the other half, what will be thought of us? We believe all they tell us about Christ's first and last coming. Why not believe *all* we are told by them that will be done on the earth? There has been enough fulfilled to prove that the author of prophecy knew the end from the beginning. All who have the Bible should understand and believe what the prophets have told us, and not let the evil spirit blind and deceive them. All men will believe this at Christ's second coming, for then he will confine the evil spirit.

At his third coming "The Lord himself *shall* descend from heaven with a shout, with the voice of the archangel, and with the trump of God; and the dead in Christ shall rise first. Then we which are alive and remain shall be caught up together with them in the clouds, to meet the Lord in the air, and so shall we ever be with the Lord." (1 Thess. 4 : 16, 17.) Then Christ will come, and bring all who have gone to heaven; and all who live on the earth then, if they are his children, will be caught up in the air with him. And all who live on the earth at that time, and are not Christ's children, will be left on the earth, and they will all be with the unrighteous dead, who will then be called from their home in the earth. For it is written that "The sea gave up the dead which were in it, and death and hell delivered up the dead which were in them; and they were judged every man according to their works. And death and hell were cast into the lake of fire. This is the second death. And whosoever was not found written in the book of life, was cast into the lake of fire." (Rev. 20 : 13 – 15.) This refers to the general judgment, and the resurrection of the righteous and unrighteous. The dead in Christ will be raised first, and will be with Christ in the air around the earth. They will witness the resurrection of those whose names were not written in the book of life. There is nothing said about bringing the lost, who are dead, to the earth, or of taking those who will be living on the earth at that time, away from the earth to meet those who have died, and will then be raised from the dead; and they could not be left on a re-created earth. "For the fearful and unbelieving, and idolaters, and all liars, shall have their part in the lake which burneth with fire and brimstone: which is the second death." (Rev. 21 : 8.)

Men may refuse to give this and other passages of God's Word which tell us the home of the lost is a lake of everlasting fire a literal interpretation, and justify themselves by saying it is impossible, for the lost could not endure it. The result of that change is, some men believe there is no future punishment. "Behold, I show you a mystery; we shall not all sleep (or die), but we shall all be changed, in a moment, in the twinkling of an eye, at the last trump;

for the trumpet shall sound, and the dead shall be raised incorruptible and we shall be changed; for this corruptible must put on incorruption, and this mortal must put on immortality; then shall be brought to pass the saying that is written, Death is swallowed up in victory." (1 Cor. 15 : 51 – 53.) "The sting of death is sin, and the strength of sin is the law. But thanks be to God which giveth us the victory through our Lord Jesus Christ." (1 Cor. 15 : 56, 57.) "For as in Adam, all die, even so in Christ shall all be made alive. Then cometh the end, when he shall have delivered up the kingdom to God, even the Father; when he shall have put down all rule and all authority and power; for he must reign till he hath put all enemies under his feet. The last enemy that shall be destroyed is death. Else what shall they do which are baptized for the dead, if the dead rise not at all ? Why are they then baptized for the dead ?" (1 Cor. 15 : 22, 26, 29) or "born of the spirit and the water." "And to you who are troubled, rest with us when the Lord Jesus shall be revealed from heaven with his mighty angels in flaming fire, taking vengeance on them that know not God, and that obey not the gospel of our Lord Jesus Christ, who shall be punished with everlasting destruction from the presence of the Lord, and from the glory of his power." (2 Thess. 1 : 7–9.)

This will all be done at Christ's third coming, and then he comes to put all his enemies under his feet, or in this earth. For then he comes as "the Lion of the tribe of Judah," to tear and rend in pieces all that would not be ruled by his law of love and mercy. He will execute judgment on the earth then, and deprive the devil of his power on the earth forever; and Christ will seal him and his up in the lake of fire forever. Then all who are not in the earth have been changed from a natural to a spiritual or an incorruptible body; for it is written, after "the resurrection they neither marry nor are given in marriage, but are as the angels of God in heaven." (Matt. 22 : 30.) Christ will not conquer death until then or after the resurrection. "When the Son of man shall come in his glory, and all the holy angels with him, then shall he sit upon the throne of his glory, and before him shall be gathered all nations." (Matt. 25 : 31, 32.) Christ is not in the third heaven then, for he has come to the earth; his throne is in the air; all the race of Adam who will be saved are with him, and all who are lost will be on the earth. For they will say "to the mountains and rocks, Fall on us and hide us from the face of him that sitteth on the throne, and from the wrath of the Lamb, for the great day of his wrath is come, and who shall be able to stand?" (Rev. 6 : 16, 17.)

This is all very plain, and we could not change the location of his throne from the air, or say all those who will be saved will not be with him, or say the lost will not go into a lake of fire. The Lord has given us this truth to instruct and warn all men.

If we do not believe this, and tell men not to believe it, we are deceiving and not warning the wicked, and "their blood will be on our skirts;" and before the end of the world the devil will deceive and make men very wicked, for we are told, "There fell upon men a great hail out of heaven, every stone about the weight of a talent, and men blasphemed God because of the plague of the hail; for the plague thereof was exceeding great." (Rev. 16 : 20, 21.) The devil must have been loosed for a long time, or the descendants of men who had lived in the time of his confinement, and had witnessed his release and the spread of sin, and could see the fruit or result of sin, would not have been so wicked. The Prophet speaks again. "And the same hour was there a great earthquake, and the tenth part of the city fell, and in the earthquake were slain of men seven thousand, and the remnant were affrighted and gave glory to the God of heaven. And the seventh angel sounded, and there were great voices in heaven, saying, The kingdoms of this world are become the kingdoms of our Lord and of his Christ, and he shall reign forever and ever." (Rev. 11 : 13–15.) At Christ's second coming he does not come to reign forever, for his reign then will be a thousand years. The city referred to must be Jerusalem, and we learn from this that wicked men will be in that city when the end comes; but some in that city will give glory to the God of heaven.

We learn from this that the affliction the Lord

sent on men before Christ's third coming was intended to be for their good. But when Christ comes finally, we are told: "A fire goeth before him, and burneth up his enemies round about. His lightnings enlightened the world; the earth saw and trembled. The hills melted like wax at the presence of the Lord, at the presence of the Lord of the whole earth." (Psa. 97 : 3–5.) All this will be done at Christ's third coming. And we are told he will " break them with a rod of iron; thou shalt dash them in pieces like a potter's vessel." (Psa. 2 : 9.) We are told, again, that "the King (or Christ) shall find out all thine enemies; thy right hand shall find out those that hate thee. Thou shalt make them as a fiery oven in the time of thine anger: the Lord shall swallow them up (in the earth) in his wrath, and the fire shall devour them. Their fruit shalt thou destroy from the earth, and their seed from among the children of men." (Psa. 21 : 8–10.) Christ did nothing like that at his first coming, and will not at his second coming; but all the above will be done at his third coming. And we are told, " The sun shall be turned into darkness, and the moon into blood, before the great and the terrible day of the Lord come." (Joel 2 : 31.) "And at that time shall Michael stand up, the great prince which standeth for the children of thy people; and there shall be a time of trouble such as never was since there was a nation, even to that same time: and at that time thy people shall be delivered, every one that shall be found written in the book. And many of them that sleep in the dust of the earth shall awake, some to everlasting life, and some to shame and everlasting contempt. And they that be wise shall shine as the brightness of the firmament, and they that turn many to righteousness as the stars forever and ever." (Dan. 12: 1–3.) The word "many" must refer to all of Adam's race, who will be saved and delivered from the power and control of the devil by the Son of God, the redeemer of our fallen race.

The Lord has told us to "Marvel not at this, for the hour is coming in the which all that are in their graves shall hear his voice, and shall come forth; they that have done good unto the resurrection of life, and they that have done evil uuto the resurrection of damnation." (John 5 : 28, 29.) This must include all the race of Adam who will ever live on the earth; some will be saved and some will be lost. And all who are saved now will be saved then. That judgment will not change what has been done. Christ has told us, "The field is the world, the good seed are the children of the kingdom: but the tares are the children of the wicked one. The enemy that sowed them is the devil, the harvest is the end of the world. And the Son of man shall send forth his angels, and they shall gather out of his kingdom all things that offend, and them which do iniquity. And shall cast them into a furnace of fire; there shall be wailing and gnashing of teeth. Then shall the righteous shine forth as the sun in the kingdom of their Father." (Matt. 13 : 38–43.) We do not treat the Holy Spirit with respect if we do not believe what is revealed to us on this subject. And Christ at his first coming repeated in plain language all that had been said in his Word about the end of the world. In speaking of the end of the world we are told, " The world that then was, being overflowed with water, perished" (2 Peter 3 : 6); that is, every living thing that was on the earth called the world did perish, except what was saved in the ark by the obedience of Noah. " But the heavens and the earth which are now, by the same word are kept in store, reserved unto fire against the day of judgment and perdition of ungodly men. The Lord is not slack concerning his promise, for one day with the Lord is as a thousand years, and a thousand years as one day. But the day of the Lord will come as a thief in the night: in the which the heavens shall pass away with a great noise, and the elements shall melt with fervent heat; the earth also, and the works that are therein, shall be burned up. Nevertheless we, according to his promise, look for new heavens and a new earth, wherein dwelleth righteousness." (2 Peter 3 : 7–13.) I do not see how we can misunderstand this language, or think prophecy could be fulfilled after this change is made on the earth, and in the air around it.

Paul has told us, " As many as have been baptized into Christ have put on Christ, and, if ye be Christ's, then are ye Abraham's seed, and heirs according to the promise." (Gal. 3 : 27–29.) And if we have the spirit of Christ we should understand and believe all he has revealed to us in his Word. Then all the promises the Lord has made to the seed of Abraham, in a future state, can be claimed by all who have put on Christ, and obey him, " For we must all appear before the judgment-seat of Christ : that every one may receive the things done, whether it be good or bad." (2 Cor. 5 : 10.) All men are judged when they die. And all who are saved will be taken by angels to heaven. And all who are lost will be left with the god of this world. And that separation is everlasting, and there will be no change made at the end of the world. " And they shall be gathered together as prisoners are gathered in the pit, and shall be shut up in the prison, and after many days shall they be visited." (Isa. 24 : 22.) And the Lord has said, if " they dig into hell thence shall mine hand take them." (Amos 9 : 2.) The lost will remain in that pit called a prison until the resurrection, and then the Lord will visit them, but he will not save or redeem them, for he will tell them to depart from him into everlasting fire prepared for the devil and his angels. The word translated "judgment-seat" means only a step or raised platform such as a person exercising any authority or pronouncing a speech might occupy. And Christ will be in the air at that time. " For as the lightning that lighteneth out of one part under heaven shineth unto the other part under heaven, so shall also the Son of man be in his day." (Luke 17 : 24.) This refers to his last coming. He does not come then in the form he was when he was parted from his apostles. He will return in that manner at his second coming. It is Antichrist who mixes those two comings in one. For Christ brings no salvation to men who live on the earth at his last coming. " If we know the truth, we should know that no LIE is the TRUTH. He that saith, I know him, and keepeth not his commandments is a liar, and the truth is not in him." (1 John 2 : 4, 21.) Christ was in the form of man when he appeared to Abraham; then he would have spared Sodom if there had been ten righteous men in that city. But his third coming will not be in that form. He does not come then to rule over men in a corruptible body.

Daniel's vision refers to his last coming. "I beheld till the thrones were cast down, and the Ancient of days did sit whose garment was white as snow, and the hair of his head like the pure wool; his throne was like the fiery flame, and his wheels as burning fire. A fiery stream issued and came forth from before him, thousand thousands ministered unto him, and ten thousand times ten thousand stood before him; the judgment was set and the books were opened. I saw, and behold, one like the Son of man came with the clouds of heaven, and came to the Ancient of days, and they brought him near before him. And there was given him dominion and glory and a kingdom, that all people, nations, and languages should serve him. His dominion is an everlasting dominion, which shall not pass away, and his kingdom that which shall not be destroyed. But the saints of the Most High shall take the kingdom and possess the kingdom forever, even forever and ever." (Dan. 7 : 9–18.) After the third coming of Christ all this will be done, and it agrees with what is said in the New Testament about Christ's last coming. And after the resurrection and the eternal separation of the wicked from the righteous, the everlasting confinement of the god of this world, the author of all sin, then the saints of the Most High will take the kingdoms of this world, with Christ for their king, and they will possess them forever and ever.

And again "Understand, O son of man; for at the time of the end shall be the vision. Behold, I will make thee know what shall be in the last end of the indignation, for at the time appointed the end shall be." (Dan. 8 : 17–19.) This end is the end of the devil's rule on the earth. The end of the multiplication of Adam's race. The end of the animal creation, and the end of all that is mortal on the earth. The end of the world as it is now. This is all very plain; and then we are told it will be called "a new heaven and a new earth, wherein dwelleth righteousness." None of this class of prophecy could refer to Christ's second coming to confine the devil for a thousand years, and then loose him from his prison to deceive the nations of the earth who are then in human form on the earth. They will obey the evil spirit and make war on their fellow-men when the devil is loosed for a season. But at the end, the first Adam will be like the second Adam, the Lord from heaven, and will be free from the power and control of the devil. Christ will free all men for a thousand years from the control of the evil spirit, while they are mortal and multiply on the earth. And he will free them forever on a new earth.

Christ is the light of the world, and all who reject Christ and do not understand his Word are blinded by "the god of this world," and are in darkness, from which flesh and blood can never deliver them. It will take the power of the Holy Spirit, that will be given in answer to believing prayer, to free them. Preaching the gospel and telling men what the Lord had done for them (while the devil is confined) will not prevent them from being deceived by him when he is loosed from his prison. For John has told us that men on the earth will be very wicked when the end comes. "By these three was the third part of men killed, by the fire and by the smoke and by the brimstone which issued out of their mouths; and the rest of the men which were not killed by these plagues yet repented not of the works of their hands, that they should not worship devils." (Rev. 9 : 18-20.) And John, speaking of the wickedness of men before the end of the age, said: " Men were scorched with great heat, and blasphemed the name of God, which hath power over these plagues: and they repented not to give him glory: and they gnawed their tongues for pain, and blasphemed the God of heaven because of their pains and their sores, and repented not of their deeds." (Rev. 16 : 9–11.) In the ninth chapter of Revelation and the second of Joel we have an account of "the angel of the bottomless pit," who will "come out of the earth with a host of evil spirits to torment men five months." They are not to kill them, but they will sting and torment them. "Their faces were as the faces of men; they had hair as the hair of women, and teeth as the teeth of lions." All this prophecy will be fulfilled after the release of the devil, and before the end of the age, or the last coming of Christ. All this will be before the time of which John speaks, when he saw the "new heaven and new earth, and the new Jerusalem, the holy city, coming down from God out of heaven, prepared as a bride adorned for her husband." It is called "the tabernacle of God with men, and he will dwell with them. And after that there will be no more death, neither sorrow, nor crying, neither shall there be any more pain; for former things are passed away. And he that sat upon the throne said, Behold, I make all things new. And he said unto me, It is done. He that overcometh shall inherit all things, and I will be his God, and he shall be my son." (Rev. 21 : 1–7.)

This does not refer to the saints ascending to heaven or coming back to the earth, but it is a temple and a city created by divine power. And it will take the place of the temple and the city that will be burned up at the end of the world or age. "And he shall send Jesus Christ, which before was preached unto you, whom the heavens must receive until the times of restitution of all things, which God hath spoken by the mouth of all his holy prophets since the world began." (Acts 3 : 20, 21.) And God said to Abraham, " In thy seed shall all the kindreds of the earth be blessed." (Acts 3 : 25.) The Lord has fulfilled so many things he has revealed to us by the prophets we can give no excuse for refusing to believe all prophecy that has not been fulfilled, for it will be fulfilled before the end of Adam's race. And we are told, " At the end of the world the angels shall come forth and sever the wicked from among the just, and shall cast them into the furnace of fire; there shall be wailing and gnashing of teeth." (Matt. 13 : 49, 50.) The Lord could not gather the Jews from all countries and plant them in their native land after that. And again we are told, " He cometh with clouds: and every eye shall see him, and they also which pierced him, and all kindreds of the earth shall wail because of him." (Rev. 1 : 7.) This must refer to his last coming, if those who pierced him when he was crucified see him and wail because of him. Men will not wail to see Christ at his second coming, for he comes then to bring peace and good-will to men, and to all that live on the earth when he comes; and that peace and good-will to men and to the Creator and to all the animal creation will continue while the evil spirit is confined.

Christ did not bring peace and good-will to men

at his first coming, and he will not at his third coming. For the evil spirit will have control of many men at his last coming. It may take the devil two thousand years from the close of the thousand years to the last coming of Christ to bring about the change the prophets say there will be in the minds of men. Again, the prophet, in speaking of his last coming, tells us " Before him shall be gathered all nations, and he shall separate them one from another as a shepherd divideth his sheep from the goats. Then shall the King say unto them on his right hand, Come, ye blessed of my Father, inherit the kingdom prepared for you from the foundation of the world. Then shall he say also unto them on the left hand, Depart from me, ye cursed, into everlasting fire, prepared for the devil and his angels." (Matt. 25 : 34-41.)

This will be at the last resurrection. The hand of mercy is withdrawn, and the judge of all the earth has come to separate the tares from the wheat, and there will be no appeal from that decision. This must include all the race of Adam who have lived on the earth, for it will be after the last resurrection, and men will not be in a human body living on the earth, for they will have a spiritual body that will live forever. Ezekiel's prophecy to the dry bones must refer to the last resurrection. It could not mean the conversion of the Jews from a spiritual death in sin to a new life in Christ, for the bones are dry, and the Lord puts flesh, sinews, and skin on them, and he puts breath in them, and they shall live; and these bones are the whole house of Israel, and the Lord has brought them up out of their graves. (Ezek. 37 : 6–9.) And those who are living then, and not in their graves (if they are Christ's children), will be caught up in the air and changed, and made like their brethren who have come with Christ from heaven. Then, and not till then, could the whole house of Israel be present. All the saved will be in the air with Christ, and the lost on the earth waiting to hear the order to " Depart from me, ye cursed, into everlasting fire."

If we attempt to change the Bible, we do it, as Peter did, at the command of Satan. When Christ told his disciples that the chief priests and scribes would kill him, and he would be raised again the third day, Peter said, " Be it far from thee, Lord; this shall not be unto thee. But Christ said to Peter, Get thee behind me, Satan; thou art an offence unto me, for thou savorest not the things that be of God, but those that be of men." (Matt. 16 : 21–24.) And Satan controlled Simon Peter when he used the sword to defend Christ, " and smote the high priest's servant and cut off his ear " (John 18 : 10); and he controlled Peter till he denied Christ, and said he did not know him. And the high priests and all who condemned Christ, the Pharisees and Sadducees, had a mold in which they molded their religious teachers, but it was not the mold that had been given to them by the prophets; and we ask, Are our theologians molded in the mold given by the prophets, if they do not believe what they have told us about Satan's home and its location, his confinement for a thousand years, his release and the spread of sin, and all the prophets have told us will be done while he is confined; also as to the third coming of Christ to raise the dead and re-create the world, and free it from sin forever? Has the Lord given us a mold in the Bible in which we could mold a teacher for all the religious denominations we have in our day? or has Satan got his theology and the Bible mixed in the minds of men?

We do not understand why the Jews do not believe what the prophets told them about Christ's first coming; and *they* do not understand why we do not believe what is revealed to us about what will be done in what we call his second coming. Satan will help men cover up any truth in the Bible that they do not want to believe. We should read the Bible and want to believe all we find in it, and not be governed by what has been handed down to us by the so-called "Fathers of the Church."

The Lord has told us to ask him for wisdom; but many think they are wise enough, and have obeyed and believed enough to save them. Some of that class are like the young man who came to Christ— almost in the kingdom; but they lack one thing, they are, like the young man and Ephraim, joined to some idol, and they will not give it up; and they would marvel if the Lord said to them, "You must 'be born of water and of the spirit, or you cannot enter into the kingdom of God.'" (John 3 : 5.) They are not willing to be as a little child and say, "Lord, save, or I perish," or, "Lord, what wilt thou have me to do?" but they are like the high priest when he said, "It is expedient for us that one man should die for the people." (John 11 : 50.)

Read what Stephen said to the men who falsely accused him, and then stoned him to death for telling them what the prophets had said Christ would do, and what he had done at his first coming. (Acts 7.) It is the same spirit that prevents men from understanding and believing what the prophets have told us he will do at his second coming. It is not a vain thing to serve and obey the Lord; and it is not a small matter to neglect or refuse to believe and obey him. It did not pay Cain when he refused to make to the Lord the right kind of an offering, and when the Lord said to him, "If thou doest well, shalt thou not be accepted? and if thou doest not well, sin lieth at the door." (Gen. 4 : 7.)

The evil spirit is the author of sin. Cain had obeyed that spirit, and was controlled by him, and would not do right. It is the same spirit who prevents men in this day from understanding and believing the Bible. Will it pay to be governed by that spirit? It did not pay King Saul to take Samuel's place and offer a burnt offering (1 Sam. 13 : 9), or to spare the oxen and the fatlings of Amalek. (1 Sam. 15 : 9.) And it did not pay the prophet who was deceived by a lying prophet, for a lion slew him on his way home. (1 Kings 13.) And it did not pay Moses when he smote the rock to say, "We," referring to himself and Aaron. It will pay to keep Christ's commands. For we are told, "He that saith, I know him, and keepeth not his commandments, is a liar, and the truth is not in him." (1 John 2 : 4.) And again we are told by Christ, "Whosoever shall break one of these least commandments, and shall teach men so, he shall be called the least in the kingdom of heaven." (Matt. 5 : 19.)

The Jews had been commanded to believe the law and the prophets. That included what had been revealed about Christ's first coming. We are to be controlled and judged by the same law. That would make it our duty to believe, and teach men to believe, all that the prophets have told us will be done for our fallen race at Christ's second coming. For it is written, "As many as have sinned without law shall also perish without law; and as many as have sinned in the law shall be judged by the law." (Rom. 2 : 12.) We have the law and all the Lord has revealed to us by the prophets. Do we believe it? Will Christ say to us as he did to his, "Friend, how camest thou in hither, not having a wedding-garment? And he was speechless." Will the king tell his "servants to cast us in outer darkness; there shall be weeping and gnashing of teeth"? (Matt. 22 : 12, 13.)

It is our duty to search the Scriptures and think over

what the Lord has said to us in his Word, and learn to believe and obey that word, and then we can have his spirit in and around us; and that will be for us a wedding-garment, and we will not then be ashamed nor speechless when we see the King or the Son of God coming. And we should remember, " The fire shall try every man's work, of what sort it is." (1 Cor. 3 : 13.) Christ's works prove his divinity, and we must believe he is able and willing to do all he has promised to do; and he has at his first coming done the most humiliating part of his work. And Christ has told us that " Heaven and earth shall pass away, but my words shall not pass away." (Matt. 13 : 31.) What does Christ mean by "passing away"? He must mean that the air and the earth, as they are now, cursed by sin, will pass away, or be changed by fire, but not consumed; for he has told us in his Word they are not to pass away. He also told us he will make " a new heaven and a new earth." He has told us all the race of Adam must die, or pass away, but in his Word he has told us they must live forever. We believe that Christ will, at his third coming, give all the race of Adam who have passed away an immortal body that will live forever, and they have one in heaven now. Then why not believe he will change this corruptible world, and the air he has created around it, to a new created matter that will remain forever? That is not as great a work as it will be to give an immortal body to all who have lived on the earth; and we must admit this, or the kingdom Christ came to establish on the earth could not be an everlasting kingdom. And he has told us in his Word that is not to pass away, the earth and his kingdom are everlasting. Then we must not give the words " pass away" a meaning we can see Christ has not given it in his Word.

The history we have of Christ in his Word he has proved to be true by his works. And he has told us before, " Till heaven and earth pass, one jot or one tittle shall in no wise pass from the law till all be fulfilled." (Matt. 5 : 18.) That must include all that he has promised to do for men, and all that live on the earth while the devil is confined; and all Christ has said will be done on the earth after the devil is released from his prison; for all that we are told will be done before the end of the world in its present form *must* and *will be* done, for his word is not to pass away till all is fulfilled. And Christ has told us " He came unto his own, and his own received him not. (John 1 : 11.) The earth is his, and that received him; but men would not.

John calls Christ "the Word of God," and he has said the " Word was with God, and the Word was God. All things were made by him, and without him was not any thing made that was made. He was in the world, and the world was made by him, and the world knew him not." (John 1 : 1, 10.) The word " world" refers to men who knew him not. " By one man sin entered into the world, and death passed upon all men." (Rom. 5 : 12.) And again we are told: "God so loved the world that he gave his only begotten Son, that whosoever believeth in him should not perish, but have everlasting life. For God sent not his Son into the world to condemn the world, but that the world through him might be saved." (John 3 : 16, 17.) In this he calls men the world. And then he has told us, "The worlds were framed by the word of God." (Heb. 11 : 3.) "By his Son, by whom also he made the worlds." (Heb. 1 : 2.) This must refer to the other planets in this solar system, worlds that were made by the Son of God; and then he tells us, "He laid the foundations of the earth that it should not be removed forever." (Psa. 104 : 5.)

What right have men to say the lake of fire in this earth, or the foundations of the earth, will be removed? How can we prove the souls of the saved will be in heaven forever, and the souls of the lost in everlasting fire forever, if we say the words "everlasting" and "forever" do not mean that when it refers to this earth? And the 21st chapter of Revelation tells us what will be done on a re-created earth: all this proves the earth must remain forever. For Christ has told us he will "reign over the house of Jacob forever, and of his kingdom there shall be no end." (Luke 1 : 33.) The kingdom and the house of Jacob over which he will rule forever will be on this earth after the house of Jacob and the earth have been re-created. And, if they are like the angels in the third heaven now, and will be like them

CHRIST'S THIRD COMING. 159

after the last resurrection, they can remain on the earth or go back to the third heaven, or in all heavens in this system.

We are told that some of the prophets have returned to the earth as angels, and those who are saved are taken to heaven by angels; and our friends who are in heaven may come to take us to heaven, when the time for our departure comes, if we are united to Christ by a living faith, and hold out to the end. All the prophets have told us what would be done at the three comings of Christ; and what they have told us would be done at his first and third coming is the beginning and end of his work. And what they have told us will be done at his second coming has not been done, and must be done before his last coming. For all who are saved then will reign with him forever, and his second coming is for a thousand years.

And to make this plain, I will repeat two verses I have quoted in what I have written about Christ's second coming: "Behold, I will bring them from the north country, and gather them from the coasts of the earth, and with them the blind and the lame, the woman with child, and her that travaileth with child together: a great company shall return thither. They shall come with weeping, and with supplications will I lead them: I will cause them to walk by the rivers of waters in a straight way, wherein they shall not stumble: for I am a father to Israel, and Ephraim is my first born." (Jere. 31 : 8, 9.) This was written six hundred and six years before Christ, and three hundred and ninety-seven years of that time the Jews had no prophet. In that time Christ was not a father to them, and they were not all his children; and at his first coming they refused to be his children, and they have refused to believe on him from that time to this. They have not come to him with weeping and supplications, and Christ has not brought them, from all the countries in which he has scattered them, to the land he gave to their fathers. That land was not in heaven, and it is not in heaven yet. But all that the prophets have told us will be done for the Jews in that land will be done, for "the Lord of hosts hath spoken it," and he changes not. And we should not find fault with the Jews for not believing Christ has come, if we do not believe he will come, as he has promised to come; nor believe he will do all he has promised to do for the Jews and for all who live on the earth at that time; for there is more prophecy to prove he will come then than there is to prove he has come, and more than there is to prove he will come the third time, to raise the dead and make all things new.

We build our church and hope of heaven on what has been promised us by Christ. The Jews do and have done the same thing. Where should our faith in what has been said about Christ begin, and where should it end? The Jews believe all that the prophets have said about what would be done at Christ's second coming; and we believe all that was said about his first coming, and all that was done by him at that coming.

And Jesus has said to us, "Be thou faithful unto death, and I will give thee a crown of life." (Rev. 2 : 10.) Christ has set us an example by doing all he was to do. And he has told us to preach his gospel to every creature, and that includes all the prophets have told us, for he has said, "Think not that I am come to destroy the law or the prophets: I am not come to destroy, but to fulfill." (Matt. 5 : 17.) If we do not give all revelation a literal interpretation we take from it all the instruction it would give to men, and then we destroy it. If our fathers have made a mistake when they explained to us the prophetic part of the Bible, we should correct that mistake.

It would cost us nothing to believe the Lord will do all he has promised to do for the Jews, and teach men to believe that class of prophecy. And all would do it if it were not for the evil spirit who deceived the Jews. This is an important question for the Gentile Church to decide. And we have no time to waste in idle meditation; for the fulfillment of prophecy, and the amount of wealth the Lord is giving the Jews, and their returning to the land the Lord has promised to them and their children, prove to us that the Lord is blessing them and preparing them for his second coming. They left Egypt and Babylon rich in this world's goods; and they could leave the nations in which they have been scattered with great wealth now.

Christ loved the Jews and wept over them; but he could not save them, for they would not believe what the prophets said about his first coming. If that was the rock which wrecked the Jewish nation, Church, and priesthood, is it safe for us to tell our children to run our Church against what is said about his second coming? Will the Holy Spirit give us any more light on this subject if we refuse to believe what the prophets (who told us about Christ's first coming) have said to us about his second coming? What will be the result? From a human stand-point, how will the members of our churches to-day compare with the Pharisees in the days of Christ? They believed Christ would come, and they believed in the resurrection of the dead: We believe he has come, and we believe in the resurrection of the dead. And Christ has told us, "Except a man be born of water and of the spirit, he cannot enter the kingdom of God." (John 3 : 5.) The meaning of the word "born" is "brought forth." If we have been sprinkled with water, have we been brought forth from a watery grave? It would be as useless for me to answer that question as it was for Paul to preach to the Jews. And again, Christ has told us if we "break one of these least commandments, and shall teach men so, we shall be called the least in the kingdom of heaven." And, again, he has said that "Except your righteousness shall exceed the righteousness of the scribes and Pharisees, ye shall in no case enter into the kingdom of heaven." (Matt. 5 : 19, 20.) The descendants of those Pharisees, and the Church of Rome, claim to be better than we are: we think we are better than they. Do we believe more of the Bible than they do? I will leave these questions for all who are interested to answer, hoping some may be taught to answer the questions in the light of revelation, "for what we do we must do quickly, for the end will soon come" to us.

I refer to the two kinds of baptism believed in and depended on in our day, to show that men cling as firmly to views they think are right now as the Jews did in the days of Christ. We can see where the Jews made a mistake better than we can see the mistakes we are making. Men may be honest in an error, but that will not make it right, and if we refuse to obey the commands of Christ, and do not believe what he has revealed to us in his Word, we make the same kind of mistake as Cain did when he changed the offering, and as the Jews did when they rejected Christ, and refused to believe what the prophets had told them about his first coming. And when Stephen proved, by the prophets they pretended to believe in, that Christ must suffer and do what he had done to fulfill prophecy, they stopped their ears, and stoned him to death.

The same evil spirit that concealed truth and prophecy from the Jews is concealing it from men in our day. Men are servants to the master they choose to obey. The Lord explained Cain's mistake to him, but he did not repent and offer the offering the Lord had commanded. Satan appealed to Christ's pride and hunger when he commanded him to turn the stones into bread. If Christ had obeyed, he would have been the devil's servant; for the law which condemned the first Adam would have condemned the second Adam; and by that law all men are to be judged. The preaching of Christ's gospel has never changed the views of the Jews, for the evil spirit has made them believe they were right; and there is no power in that gospel to change the views of men now, if they do not believe it, and are not willing to be governed by it. Men are willing to believe Christ's promises, and they are willing to receive the reward; but they do not want to obey his commands if they think something else will do as well.

We learn from this that, if men do not believe what the prophets have told us about the home of the lost, the second coming of Christ to confine the devil, his release, the spread of sin, Christ's third coming to raise the dead and make all things new, it is the evil spirit who hides it from them; for he has always been working on that line, and he has in all ages of the world controlled men to a greater or less extent. But when he is confined for a thousand years, all on the earth will be free from his power and control; and when he is loosed from his prison for a season he will deceive men who live on the earth, and they will serve and obey him; and the prophets have told us what the result of that mistake will be. We are told what the evil spirits, who come out of the earth, will do to that class of men: And the Lord " commanded them not to hurt the grass of the earth, neither any green thing, neither any tree, but only those men which have *not* the seal of God in their foreheads." (Rev. 9 : 4.) There will be men living on the earth then who fear and serve the Lord, and he will protect them.

All this must be fulfilled on this earth before the third coming of Christ to make all things new, and confine the devil and all who are his of the race of Adam, with the angels who were driven with him from heaven, into the lake of fire in this earth forever. The prophets have made this very plain, and the meaning of the words used will not permit us to explain it in any other way; for good and bad men live on the earth then, and the devil and his host come from the earth to torment the men who do not fear the Lord and keep his commandments. " By these three was the third part of men killed, by the fire, and by the smoke, and by the brimstone which issued out of their mouths." (Rev. 9 : 18.)

This locates the home of Satan and the lost, and teaches us what will be done by them on the earth before the end comes; and they are on the earth at his last coming, and there is nothing said about taking them away then. Why should we think they will be taken away from the earth? Some may think this is not to be understood by the meaning of the words used. Why not? We believe and explain all the prophets tell us about Christ's first coming, by the meaning of the words used, and we understand all he has promised to do for us in the same way, and all he has told us to do for him, and then refuse to believe what is said about his second coming, as the Jews refuse to believe what is revealed to them about his first coming. Christ can include the Gentiles with the Jews when he says, "Oh ye of little faith." We may ask, Why is this? The best answer I can give is, self-interest and the interest the evil spirit has in persuading men not to believe the Bible as it has been written by the prophets to instruct men in all ages.

Some may think I should not differ so much from those who are called the wise men of this age when I explain the Bible. Christ and his Apostles had to differ from the wise men who lived in that day; and the plain truth has never been popular with men. And yet the past proves it has paid all men and nations to believe and obey all the Lord has revealed to them. It never has paid men to believe what suits them, and refuse to believe the rest of God's truth. Then we should be wise in our day, and, if we would have wisdom, we must believe all that has been revealed to us by the author of all wisdom. Men in all ages of the world have refused to believe many things the Lord had revealed to them, and the result of that mistake is recorded in the Bible for our instruction. Are we profiting by it? Many who live in this day are not, and they can never blame the Lord for it.

The first promise the Lord made to our fallen race was that the seed of woman in the person of Christ would "bruise the serpent's head," and the "serpent shall bruise his heel." (Gen. 3:15.) At Christ's first coming the old serpent, or Satan, bruised Christ's heel, but Christ did not bruise the serpent's head. For before that coming men were saved from the power and control of Satan by believing Christ would come, and by obeying other commands the Lord had given them. When Christ came, he changed the promise and told all men they must believe he had come, and must obey the commands he gave them, or they could not be saved. The old serpent controlled the Jews, and they would not believe nor obey the commands. Then the serpent bruised Christ's heel, for his people and kindred refused to believe on him, and would not give up the old promises that Christ told them he would take from them and give them a new covenant. That change proved to be a curse and not a blessing to them. Look over the history of the Gentile Church for one thousand three hundred years from that time; then look at the discord and division there has been in the Church of Christ from the Reformation to this time, and can we say this new dispensation has bruised the old serpent's head more than the old dispensation did? And if this state of things continue till the end of the age, or the third coming of Christ to confine the old serpent forever, that bruising of the serpent's head will do our race no good; for they will not multiply on the earth after that, and all will be saved or lost then, and the devil's work on earth will end forever.

At Christ's SECOND coming he will bruise the old serpent's head when he confines him and his "in a bottomless pit for a thousand years, so he cannot deceive the nations of the earth till the thousand years are ended." Then Christ will fulfill that promise, and not till then. And all men who live on the earth in that time will be saved. Christ is called the light of the world. Have we that light if we refuse to believe what he has told us about his second coming, the confinement of the devil, and Christ's peaceful and sinless reign over all the nations of the earth, and over all the animal creation for a thousand years with those who will have part in the first resurrection? Also the release of the devil and the spread of sin before his last coming; and then, if we do not believe what he has told us about the home of the lost, and its location, and refuse to give a literal interpretation to what he has told us about the third heaven, called paradise and Christ's kingdom, do we believe more prophecy than the Jews do?

We accept the sacrifice made by Christ for sin. That is the foundation for our hope, and it is a safe foundation; but we should, by our faith and works, build on it and believe all revelation. Some of our theologians tell us they do not know that paradise is heaven. They would know it if they would believe what is revealed; for Paul has told us he was "caught up to the third heaven," and he was then in paradise, and Christ called it his kingdom. The variety of explanations given to plain statements made in the Word of God, that we could understand if we would explain them as we do the passages of Scripture we believe, proves some must be mistaken. If all who think they are on the road to heaven are on the road marked out in the Bible, it must be the broad road that leads to heaven, and the narrow road that leads to hell, and few there be that find it. Very few will think they are on the wrong road, but they will believe many others are. We have been taught to believe that Christ has rejected and scattered the Jews because they refused to believe what the prophets had told them about Christ's first coming; and the prophets tell us that is the reason they have been rejected. If the Gentile Church, with all its branches, are to be judged by that rule by the Judge who condemned the Jews for not believing his word, will all the Gentiles who claim to be Christians receive the reward?

The Holy Spirit will give all Christians wisdom enough to answer that question, and to understand and believe the Bible, if they want the instruction. But many of the Gentile Christians are like the Jews: they think they know and believe enough to take them to heaven, and they do not WANT to know any more. ALL Christians should free themselves from that bondage, for Satan is controlling many of our race in that way. They are almost in the kingdom, and he makes them believe they are all right, but he knows they are not. The evil spirit has persuaded many men to persecute the Church of Christ, and made them believe they were doing God's service. I think all will admit this; and many should profit by it. And in writing this book I think I have done what the Lord has called me to do, and think it will help all those who want instruction, to understand the prophetic part of the Bible, and help them to believe what the Lord has revealed to us in his Word. I have tried to explain all prophecy in the same way we have been taught to explain part of it, by the meaning of the words used to instruct men who live on the earth. I have received no new revelation, and have only drawn a true picture of what is revealed to us in the Word of God, by which all men must be judged. And if the explanation I have given is not a true one in some points, it is better than *no* explanation of that part of the Bible; but I think it is true.

I know of nothing more suitable to close this with than the prayer of Jesus, when he said: "I thank thee, O Father, Lord of heaven and earth, because thou hast hid these things from the wise and prudent, and hast revealed them unto babes." (Matt. 11 : 25.) And we are to give up our wisdom and become as little children, and depend on the wisdom the Lord has promised to give us if we want it.

CHRIST'S THIRD COMING.

1. Men must live in a future state,
    In heaven or eternal woe ;
   And in the end all men must reap
    The crop they in this life did sow.

2. Men should believe what is revealed,
    For as our faith, our strength shall be:
   We are in bondage here on earth—
    The Lord is pleased to make us free.

3. Then think of the songs which are sung
    By angels and saints up on high:
   Oh, think of that beautiful home
    That is up in the bright blue sky;

4. And then think of our Father's love;
    The sacrifice made by his Son;
   Of all he has promised to do;
    Of all that by him has been done.

5. We should love the Father and Son,
    The Spirit, our Comforter too,
   If we are united with them
    By a work God's spirit will do;

6. If we love, believe, and obey
    All the Lord has commanded ;
   And that is what all men should do,
    For that God's law has demanded.

7. Oh, think of the home of the lost,
    It is worse than feeding the swine;
   Far better to feed on the husks
    Than on fire and brimstone to dine.

8. He spared not the angels who sinned—
   Can we ask him to save our race
   If they do not obey his Word?
   Will the Lord save them by his grace?

9. He has told us he never will.
   Believe it or not, as we choose;
   Then we will have no one to blame
   If Heaven forever we lose.

10. Then think of the good we could do,
    Of friends we are leading astray;
    Oh, repent and believe his Word,
    And come to the Saviour to-day.

A REVIEW OF THE SUBJECTS IN VERSE.

1. The earth was made three days before
     God made the moon and sun;
   The day and night did not commence
     Until the sun was done.

2. The devil makes some men believe
     The earth came from the sun
   All in a melted mass of fire,
     And stopped here on its run.

3. I do not think they ever tell
     What stopped it in its flight,
   Or keeps it moving around the sun,
     Or how the sun gives light.

4. If all the planets in second heaven
     Were thrown off from the sun,
   How could God say he made the earth
     Before he made the sun?

5. The Father and his only Son
     Were in heaven number three,
   Before earth, sun, and moon were made,
     Or water in the sea;

6. Before the depths of hell were made,
     Before the devil fell
   From heaven to the earth below,
     Where he at present dwells.

7. One word from God did form earth's walls
    Of rocks and mica stone
  Around the devil's fiery host,
    When driven from heaven, their home.

8. Attraction would not let the world,
    If melted, leave the sun;
  For water does not leave the earth,
    And it's moving with the sun.

9. If melted worlds could leave the sun,
    The sun would soon be scattered,
  A million worlds would fly in space;
    All would be torn and tattered.

10. The law of attraction would be gone,
    If worlds could leave the sun.
  The water then would leave the earth,
    And to the third heaven run.

11. The Lord is in unbounded space;
    On earth and in the air,
  In the bottomless pit of hell—
    The Lord is everywhere.

12. Some think the devil is not bound
    To stay in earth and air,
  But think he goes from earth to hell,
    And then roams anywhere.

13. Some think that heaven and hell are up;
    Or think that they must *leave*
  This earth and air to find the place
    Called upper and lower Hades.

14. That is not in the Word of God;
    The devil tells that lie;
  For heaven is up and hell is down;
    He has no home on high.

15. The air that's all around the earth
    Is called heaven number one:
  In space called heaven number two
    It's moving around the sun.

16. For in that heaven number two,
    Earth, sun, and moon do go;
  As the Creator of all things
    Has ordered them, we know.

17. All second heaven is empty space.
    Then heaven number three;
  All of that heaven is paradise,
    There all God's saints will be.

18. The heavens above are all for heights,
    Earth beneath is for depths;
  Go to the centre of this earth,
    That is the end of depths.

19. The saints and the angelic host
    Are all around the earth,
  Watching the devil and all men.
    They know what heaven is worth.

20. There is joy in heaven when a soul
    From sin has turned away,
  And has become a child of God;
    He protects him every day.

21. The heavens above, God made for right;
    The earth beneath, for sin.
    The heavens above are all in sight,
    Earth beneath is unseen.

22. The word heaven means, to "heave up"
    From this, the earth below;
    And hell means, in a covered place,
    And must be concealed, we know.

23. The heavens above are all God's throne,
    The devil is god of earth.
    The Lord will come from heaven, his throne,
    To chain the devil *in* earth.

24. The devil, then, a thousand years
    Must in earth's prison stay;
    God's Son will rule all nations then,
    And protect them night and day.

25. All he has promised to the Jews
    Will then by him be done;
    For it was promised to their fathers
    By God, the *Father*, and his *Son*.

26. At the end of the thousand years,
    The devil will be loosed again;
    He will deceive all nations then,
    While *this*, a sinful world, remains.

27. And when that sinful age shall end,
    Then the Son of God will come
    To confine the devil forever,
    In earth, his eternal home.

28. The hills will be melted like wax;
   But he makes all things new.
  The Lord will come to raise the dead;
   The Gentile and the Jew.

29. The devil was driven from heaven to earth.
   As lightning he did fall;
  No place, in space called heaven, for him;
   No saving him or his at all.

30. Hell is a lake of fire in earth;
   It's the prison for the lost.
  God's elect are in heaven above;
   The blood of Christ it cost.

31. Hell is in a bottomless pit;
   The lower parts of earth,
  In which the souls of all must go
   Who have not the new birth.

32. Hell is a prison in the earth,
   In which the lost must be;
  The mountains form the prison walls,
   The Lord, he has the key.

33. That pit God calls outer darkness;
   For in its prison walls
  The sun of heaven never shines,
   To light its gloomy halls.

34. Stephen, from earth to heaven, saw
   The Son of God on high.
  He did not see the devil there,
   Exalted with him in the sky.

35. The rich man from the pit called hell,
    Could see to heaven, too;
From an opening in the earth,
    Saw Abraham, and Lazarus too.

36. The power of God could fix a gulf
    Around this part of space
That would keep the lost from heaven,
    As well as any other place.

37. If hell is not in earth below,
    How could God say it's down;
Or fix a gulf they could not pass
    The devil's home around.

38. This world is called the devil's home;
    Has he a home on high
To which he sends the souls of those
    Who in his service die?

39. How could the devil get them there?
    Who guides them on the way,
And keeps them from the saints above,
    If hell is so far away?

40. The devil could not leave the earth,
    For he must watch his prey;
For men would serve the Lord
    If he was gone away.

41. When Christ and his elect do come,
    From his throne on high,
To raise the dead, and judge all men,
    Who brings the *lost* to earth to die?

42. They must be up in space called heaven,
      If not in earth confined,
    And come with Christ and his elect.
      How can that be denied?

43. The power of the Son of God
      Will shine from pole to pole;
    Angels and saints with him in air,
      Will the lost on earth control.

44. If in the pit of hell they dig,
      His hand shall take them out;
    For they must look on him they pierced
      When the Archangel shouts.

45. Then some are taken up in air,
      And others left on earth.
    The mountains, they will hide them from
      The Lord of heaven and earth.

46. For then the Lord will seal them up
      In the dark pit called hell;
    Then all who serve the devil here
      Must with him ever dwell.

47. That is called the second death,
      From which none are redeemed;
    They, with the devil in hades,
      Must ever be concealed.

48. Some think there is not room in earth,
      For all the lost in time;
    Legion of devils in *one* man
      Controlled two thousand swine.

49. If a man in an iron house
    Should die of suffocation,
  The soul would leave that iron ball
    With no hesitation.

50. God's chamber is eight thousand miles
    From one side to the other.
  And there is room enough in that;
    He will make no other.

51. Some think the soul could not endure
    The fire that is in earth;
  The Lord who saved from fire on earth
    Knows what his power is worth.

52. The Lord has made a fire in earth:
    Since he has made it there,
  Why make another fire in space,
    And send the lost up there?

53. Why should we think that hell is up?
    The Lord says it is down;
  To leave this earth is going up
    From *all* the *world around*.

54. He *could* have said there was a hell
    With prison walls around;
  And went on to describe the place,
    And not said it was down.

55. Is there a pit in heaven above,
    With prison walls around?
  And in that pit of fire and smoke
    No bottom can be found?

A REVIEW OF THE SUBJECTS IN VERSE. 181

56. If not, there is a pit in earth,
    With fire and smoke below;
The earth's crust is the prison walls.
    Is there a bottom? No.

57. If hell is not in earth below,
    How could we dig in it,
Go down in it, or how could we
    Ascend out of the pit?

58. If hell is up in space called heaven,
    Why does God say it's down?
If it is not in earth below,
    No other place is found,

59. Except the sun and moon and stars,
    In heaven number two;
But then we must go up to them,
    And that would never do.

60. If *men* had told us hell was down
    There *could* be some mistake;
The *Lord* has told it in his Word;
    Can we *that* underrate?

61. The Bible says that heaven is up,
    And down comes to the earth;
If hell is up in space called heaven,
    What is the Bible worth?

62. If a false statement can be found
    In this, the Word of God,
Can he be just if he applies
    For sin the chastening rod?

63. The bodies of all Pharaoh's host
    Sank in the raging sea;
  Their souls were swallowed by the earth
    And there must ever be.

64. Nine hundred years from that event,
    Pharaoh was in the earth;
  And he was comforted to know
    The Jews knew what hell was worth.

65. All go to sheol or the grave;
    There is no knowledge there;
  The mind has left that house of clay,
    Gone? ask the Bible where.

66. God's angels carried Lazarus
    To heaven, far away;
  The rich man died, went down in hell;
    For he in earth did stay.

67. So I with Shakespeare, then, would say:
    "Death is the fatal knell
  That soon will summons all mankind,
    To heaven or to hell."

68. Jonah was swallowed by a fish;
    His soul fainted in him;
  Then to the bottom of the sea
    With the weeds about him.

69. To the bottom of the mountains,
    Then Jonah's soul did go;
  With the bars of earth about him,
    In hell, eternal woe.

70. Then from this earth, called hell's belly,
      To the Lord did Jonah cry;
    For he was in the pit of hell,
      Not in heaven on high.

71. And the fish cast Jonah's body
      From its mouth on dry land;
    His soul returned to it from hell,
      His body then could stand.

72. Then Jonah went to Nineveh,
      And he obeyed the Lord;
    He told them, in that great city,
      To repent, or be destroyed.

73. They believed the words of Jonah,
      The Lord forgave them all:
    Jonah was with the Lord displeased,
      Who saved them from the fall.

74. Paul up to the third heaven went;
      Christ and the thief went there;
    Christ returned, and to Mary said
      His Father was not there.

75. This would be all right and proper,
      The Lord, the great I AM,
    To be above and all around
      The devil and fallen man.

76. Yet in spirit he is present
      In all unbounded space,
    Controlling all the host of heaven
      And all our helpless race.

77. The angel comes from heaven to earth
   With orders, and the key
  To open the bottomless pit
   And let its inmates free.

78. Leader of the fallen angels
   Five months on earth must be,
  To sting and then torment all men
   That Christ has not made free.

79. Men will seek death; but it will flee
   From them in their distress.
  But they would not repent and seek
   The Lord, so he could bless.

80. The smoke arose out of the pit,
   Till the air was darkened
  By the smoke of this earth's furnace;
   But men's hearts were hardened.

81. We cannot from his presence flee
   If we in *hell* do go;
  For *there* God's controlling power
   Will keep his bitter foe.

82. The devil had control of Saul
   And the witch at Endor.
  And he, to let Saul know his fate,
   Told him to go to Endor.

83. The gods ascending from the earth
   Told her the fate of Saul.
  The *devil* wanted *Saul* to think,
   That *Samuel said* it all.

84. And on the morrow Saul must go
   In this earth's pit to see
The devil he had served so well.
   For Saul must be with *me*.

85. So said the devil and the witch;
   To-morrow Saul must die,
And then his soul will be with me
   In hell, and not on high.

86. Elijah went up to heaven in fire—
   The chariot of the Lord.
Korah went down alive in the pit.
   He disobeyed God's word.

87. Korah did not go up to heaven
   From that, the pit of hell;
Or leave this earth to find a home
   Where devils did not dwell.

88. For he with all the lost, I think,
   Must with the devil stay,
In that fire prepared for devils,
   Until the Judgment Day.

89. Why was the devil driven to earth,
   And left here till this day?
Why come and seal him in the pit,
   And not take him away?

90. What is this in the Bible for,
   If we are not to know
Where *is* and *was* the devil's home,
   And where he is to go?

91. If he came from heaven to earth,
    And is and has been here,
And is to be sealed up in earth,
    Need those in heaven fear?

92. If the devil and the lost must be
    Taken from this their home,
Why has not the Word of God
    Told us where they must roam?

93. When God speaks of unbounded space
    It's heaven, earth, and hell;
And if there is another place
    He has not thought to tell.

94. How could the lost come back to earth
    On the last Judgment Day,
If hell is up in space, called heaven,
    From earth so far away?

95. How could the devil and his host
    Pass Christ's host in the air?
Which they must do if not in earth,
    And they are anywhere.

96. Depart from me, ye cursed ones,
    In everlasting fire;
Because you would not obey me,
    You can go no higher.

97. How came you in my Church on earth
    Without my spirit's robe?
You must have on that robe of light;
    Or leave my saints' abode.

98. Take him and bind him in the grave;
    His hands and feet and all;
   Send his soul in outer darkness
    To weep for sin, the fall.

99. "The Church on earth is my Son's Bride,
    They are conceived by him
   That enter in my Church above;"
    So says the great I AM.

100. If Christ is not your living head,
    The devil is your guide;
   And he will blind your eye of faith,
    Till you in hell will hide.

101. And when Christ takes you from that pit,
    To judge you for the crime
   Of not believing on his name
    While you were here in time;

102. And when you see him in his power,
    You will return to hell;
   Then the earth's walls will hide you.
    With him you could not dwell.

103. If three heavens surround the earth,
    The devil here must stay;
   With the angelic host in heaven,
    He could not get away.

104. Are we not trifling with our King
    To disbelieve one-third,
   And say we do not understand
    The meaning of his word?

105. When all the words are very plain,
    And we know what they mean;
  And all God's writers do agree,
    As can be plainly seen.

106. Down in the lower parts of earth,
    With graves around the pit,
  All covered and concealed from men—
    Plain words as he could get.

107. All we know of heaven or hell,
    We must learn from God's Book;
  And we, on those sacred pages,
    Are commanded to look.

108. And if we do not understand
    What God has there revealed,
  It is because of unbelief
    Those truths are all concealed.

109. Then let us on those pages look
    With a believing mind;
  It's the only way to honor
    The Lord who is so kind.

110. And we must not change the meaning
    Of words that he employs;
  For the devil is the author
    Of all that would destroy

111. The meaning of what is revealed
    In this, the Book that's given
  To lead us from the power of sin
    Up to the court of heaven.

112. "Thou thunder with a voice like him,
    Hast thou an arm like God?
   Deck thyself with majesty,
    And look on one that's proud."

113. Well may the God of heaven be proud,
    For he has none to fear;
   He reigns and rules in heaven and hell,
    No rival or a peer.

114. How condescending in our God
    To speak to mortal man
   In language so sublime and grand,
    The Lord, the great I AM.

115. He breathed in man eternal life,
    And that he calls the soul;
   That must forever live in heaven,
    Or be in hell controlled.

116. If what the Lord has ordered said
    In this, the Word of God,
   Is not the truth, the devil would
    Have told the Son of God,

117. When he was tempting him, that what
    Was written about hell
   Did not describe the place where he
    And his must ever dwell.

118. The Lord has given us this truth,
    The devil don't find fault;
   We could not change it if we would.
    Then why make the assault?

119. Or say we do not understand
　　　What all God's writers say,
　　About hell and it's location,
　　　But think it's far away?

120. The earth's foundation has been laid
　　　With God's almighty hand;
　　No power will move those giant walls,
　　　They must forever stand.

121. God to the raging sea has said,
　　　" Here thy proud waves must stay."
　　The sea obeys the Lord's command,
　　　And will till Judgment Day.

122. This world obeys the Word of God;
　　　Yields fruit in every clime;
　　But man, poor silly man, rebels,
　　　And will not obey in time.

123. The good and bad together live,
　　　Wheat and tares together grow,
　　'Till God's appointed reaper comes
　　　To take the good to heaven, his home.

124. Then, like the chaff, the bad will burn,
　　　In earth's eternal fire,
　　With all that helped deceive them,
　　　With the father of a liar.

125. Devils will tremble and believe
　　　That he is Lord of all.
　　All keees will bow, and tongues confess,
　　　That he controls them all,

126. In heaven, hell, and on the earth,
　　　And in the raging sea;
　　For all that ever lived in time
　　　Must in his presence be.

127. The unseen power around the earth
　　　Must be the power of God;
　　With his electric power above,
　　　None can escape his rod.

128. Oh hear the sad cry of the lost!
　　　It comes from a lake of fire;
　　Oh repent and believe the truth—
　　　Do what the Lord doth require.

129. If David could not trifle with
　　　The God who made him king;
　　But trusted in the arm of man
　　　That no protection brings.

130. When David numbered all his men,
　　　It was a foolish thing;
　　The Lord told David he had sinned,
　　　And offered him three things.

131. David fell in the hands of God,
　　　And seventy thousand men
　　Fell by the angel's sword of death.
　　　David repented then.

132. The God of heaven changes not;
　　　He will not change forever;
　　Then all the Bible is his word,
　　　And will not change; no, never!

133. That lamp of light will guide us
    From this abode of sin,
Up to heaven and to glory,
    Where we will be like him.

134. And when we get up to heaven,
    If ordered *down* to earth,
If we do not understand him,
    What would he think us worth?

135. We had ascended from the earth;
    That every one would know;
And to return, we must come down:
    That would be the way to go.

136. Leave this earth would mean " go up,"
    No other meaning could be found;
The centre of this earth would *mean*,
    And *must be* the end of down.

137. Some think there is no local hell,
    And not a lake of fire
That is a prison for the lost,
    But want to look up higher.

138. Why think there is a local heaven
    Up from the earth in space?
Because the Bible says there is,
    And then describes the place.

139. The Bible says there is a hell—
    Locates it in the earth—
Called a pit without a bottom—
    What is that statement worth?

140. The description we have of hell
    Is plainer than that of heaven;
We can find it in the Bible,
    Given by the God of heaven.

141. If we believe there is heaven,
    Why not believe in hell?
If not, the devil and all the lost
    Will go to heaven as well.

142. If we believe that hell is down,
    And air, called heaven, around it,
Then why go up through heaven to find
    Hell that's down below it?

143. Is that believing all we find
    In this, the Word of God?
Can we go on and change his Word,
    And then escape his rod?

144. Faith is the only key that's given
    That opens to the mind
The meaning of the Word of God—
    The only way we find

145. To please the God of heaven and earth;
    He will then his Spirit give
To all who will believe his Word—
    They, with him, can ever live.

146. Then unbelief will close the eyes
    That faith to us would give;
In darkness, not in light, we go;
    While here on earth we live.

147. Then how can we love the Author
     Of all that's good and true?
   He cannot look on unbelief,
     And love and honor you.

148. And faith will keep us from all harm,
     For then we in Christ can live,
   In him and he will live in us,
     And he will his spirit give.

149. When the spirit of the Son of God
     From Peter was withdrawn,
   The devil had control of him,
     And he denied the Lord.

150. If those who read this little book
     Think hell is not in earth;
   Have you the spirit of God's Son?
     If you *have*, what is it worth?

151. Jesus asked Peter, "Who am I?"
     "The Son of God," was his reply.
   That, by flesh, was not revealed to thee;
     But by God's spirit from on high.

152. Are we all willing to be taught
     By the spirit of God's love,
   Or do we love men's instruction,
     More than God's spirit from above?

153. If we to *men's* traditions cling,
     Not to God's spirit from on *high;*
   That looks like the devil's work—
     To Eve: "Thou shalt not surely die."

154. "Search the Scripture," is Christ's command,
     To learn what we must do.
   That word will give eternal life,
     If you do not misconstrue

155. The meaning of plain words that's used,
     If the devil tells us what
   The Word of God would have us do;
     Obey the devil! Oh, do not.

156. Millions of our fallen race to-day,
     Take the devil's explanation
   Of commands the Lord has given.
     It *may* bring them condemnation.

157. We should be sure we're right,
     For mistakes are not corrected,
   And in the future world, you know,
     They are sure to *be* detected.

158. The command to Cain and Abel
     Was an offering to the Lord.
   The devil came and said to Cain,
     "Change the offering and God's Word."

159. Cain did obey the devil then,
     And was then by him controlled,
   Till he his righteous brother slew;
     Then Cain was to the devil sold.

160. His punishment was not in life;
     But in a future state;
   His punishment he could not bear,
     When the *Lord* told him his fate.

161. Cain with the devil is in earth;
    Will forever be in it;
    With the devil and all the lost
    In a bottomless pit.

162. Hell and the grave is called a pit,
    And a prison for the soul.
    They are a prison, and conceal
    The body and the soul.

163. The Hebrew for hell is sheol;
    The same word for the grave.
    Christ's soul was not left here in hell,
    Or his body in the grave.

164. Then hell must be in earth below,
    And not in heaven above;
    Sin and a lie cannot go there;
    Heaven is truth and love.

165. The devil has sowed many tares,
    That're growing in the minds of men;
    They believe they are God's children,
    But *that* they have never been.

166. They may think they cast out devils,
    In Christ's name do many works:
    Christ's spirit does not do the work;
    In them the evil spirit lurks.

167. Christ has said he never knew them,
    And tells them they must depart.
    How *many* are among that number
    Who has not had a new heart?

168. I say you *must* be born again,
   Of spirit, and the water too—
  Thus saith the Son of God to us—
   If my commands you wish to do.

169. If the hand of persecution
   Should on the Church be laid,
  How many, like false Peter, would
   Answer the accusing maid.

170. This book, like Bunyan's, is God's gift
   To this, his Church below,
  And will be yet believed by them
   Who will to heaven go.

171. Its author is not trained by men,
   In any earthly school,
  To understand theology,
   But trained by God's own rule.

172. That rule is faith in all we find
   In this, the book of God,
  That tells us how we may escape
   From his correcting rod.

173. The reformers did a noble work;
   Is that all we can find
  In a book that has an author
   With an eternal mind?

174. Look at the fields of earthly fame,
   Of science, and of art;
  They, of the Church of Christ, have got
   About fifty years the start.

175. This truth is hid from men that's wise,
     And is revealed to one,
   Whom he has called to do the work
     That he has wanted done.

176. The wisdom of the Son of God
     Was questioned by wise men;
   And many things that's new and true
     Have been opposed by them.

177. No new invention has been made,
     Wise men at first receive,
   Until it's all completed,
     They are forced to believe.

178. What if men, like Saul of Tarsus,
     Who are trained in this age,
   At the feet of our Gamaliel,
     Should all be in a rage,

179. If the Lord should tell a farmer
     To tell them they could find
   Some truths in the Word of God,
     That have escaped their mind?

180. And the minds of the reformers,
     Whose judgment they believe,
   Is good in all theology,
     And that they will receive.

181. I will say to wordly wise men,
     If you will stop and think,
   There is a power on God's throne,
     His truth will never sink.

182. If inventors had been controlled
    By the minds of other men,
 Who did not understand the power
    Of invention and the pen,

183. Would we have had the use of steam,
    And all the works of art,
 The printing-press and telegraph,
    That gives men a new start?

184. Then let Theology improve,
    If in God's Book is found
 Material on which to build,
    That is on solid ground.

185. The Lord will then endorse the work,
    And none can overthrow;
 For all his word must be fulfilled,
    This he does plainly show.

186. Must we fear man who has no power
    But to destroy this clay,
 When God has power to cast in hell
    The soul, where it must stay?

187. Give me the Bible as it is,
    You may take all the rest;
 For it has God for its author,
    And his Word is the best.

188. The Bible tells us heaven is up,
    And hell is down in earth;
 If *men* say hell is up from earth
    What is *their* story worth?

189. For they have not been up to see,
 Or down in hell, you know;
 And if we leave the Word of God,
 Who knows the way to go?

190. And why have hell in space above?
 What reason can they give?
 Angels go in all space called heaven;
 With them saints *will* ever live.

191. God's angels come from the third heaven,
 Through heaven number two;
 To air, called heaven, around the earth
 They came God's will to do.

192. If men would only stop and think
 Of all God has revealed
 In the Bible and by his Son,
 This truth is not concealed.

193. All the men who wrote the Bible,
 Would not think hell was down,
 Till God's Holy Spirit told them
 The pit, called hell, was down.

194. This would not be the devil's work:
 He would not let men know
 That all who serve him here on earth
 Must in it ever go.

195. If the author of the Bible
 Has ordered it revealed,
 Why should men, who claim to love him,
 Try to keep it concealed?

196. If the spirit that doth lead us
   Is leading us away
From plain truths that's in the Bible,
   He is leading us astray.

197. That spirit is the evil one,
   To that spirit we must not go
To learn the way of truth and right;
   To all truth he is a foe.

198. That spirit would not let the Jews
   Believe the Son of God;
That spirit cannot free them from
   The Lord's controlling rod.

199. If men will not believe this truth
   It will not change the place;
That for the devil God has made,
   And all who refuse his grace.

200. Reader, you may my work condemn,
   But do not condemn *God's Word*,
Or, when the shades of *death* draw nigh,
   Your prayer of *fear* will not be *heard*.

THE END.